D1525837

OBAMA AT WAR

OBAMA AT WAR

CONGRESS AND THE
IMPERIAL PRESIDENCY

Ryan C. Hendrickson

UNIVERSITY PRESS OF KENTUCKY

Scholarly publisher for the Commonwealth,
serving Bellarmine University, Berea College, Centre College of Kentucky,
Eastern Kentucky University, The Filson Historical Society, Georgetown College,
Kentucky Historical Society, Kentucky State University,
Morehead State University, Murray State University, Northern Kentucky
University, Transylvania University, University of Kentucky, University of
Louisville, and Western Kentucky University.
All rights reserved.

Editorial and Sales Offices: The University Press of Kentucky
663 South Limestone Street, Lexington, Kentucky 40508-4008
www.kentuckypress.com

Library of Congress Cataloging-in-Publication Data

Hendrickson, Ryan C., 1969–
  Obama at war : Congress and the imperial presidency / Ryan C. Hendrickson.
    pages cm
  Includes bibliographical references and index.
  ISBN 978-0-8131-6094-8 (hardcover : acid-free paper) —
  ISBN 978-0-8131-6096-2 (PDF) — ISBN 978-0-8131-6095-5 (ePub)
  1. Obama, Barack—Military leadership. 2. United States—Military policy.
3. United States—Military policy—Case studies. 4. United States—Foreign
relations—2009– 5. War and emergency powers—United States. 6. United
States. Congress—History—21st century. 7. Kerry, John, 1943– 8. McCain,
John, 1936– I. Title.
  E908.3.H46 2015
  973.932092—dc23   2015000736

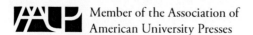

For my wife, Tece

Contents

Introduction

Red Lines for War

President Barack Obama faced a major foreign-policy challenge and humanitarian crisis in 2012 as civil war raged in Syria. As Syrian president Bashar al-Assad continued his slaughter of governmental insurgents, Obama attempted to show the world that his military strength and diplomatic resolve vis-à-vis Syria was genuine. As many commanders in chief have done since the Second World War, on August 20, 2012, Obama created his own "red line" for Assad's behavior that would potentially result in U.S. military intervention. His message to the Syrian leader was clear: "We have been very clear to the Assad regime, but also to other players on the ground, that a red line for us is we start seeing a whole bunch of chemical weapons moving around or being utilized. That would change my calculus. That would change my equation."[1]

In a similar vein, on April 11, 2010, with increased concerns over Iran's and North Korea's unwillingness to cooperate with the United States and the United Nations (UN) on a host of nuclear-proliferation issues, Obama's then secretary of defense Robert Gates discussed the threat that each state posed to the United States. His foreign-policy message was not difficult to decipher: "Because North Korea and Iran are not in compliance with the Nuclear Nonproliferation Treaty . . . for them, all bets are off. All options are on the table."[2] On Iran and its ongoing nuclear weapons program, in 2013 Obama reiterated his administration's policy: "If we can resolve it diplomatically, that's a more lasting solution. If not, I continue to keep all options on the table. . . . When I say all options are on the table, all options are on the table. The United States has significant capabilities."[3]

Though today it may sound normal for a president to threaten and potentially use military force abroad—as the Obama presidency has done to three different countries—such views would have been especially abhorrent to American Founding Father Elbridge Gerry from Massachusetts at the Constitutional Convention in 1787. Gerry, whose views won out over a call for an empowered commander in chief at the convention, noted that he "never expected to hear in a republic a motion to empower the Executive alone to declare war."[4] Today, to American commanders in chief and many leaders of Congress, Gerry's views are not even a distant memory but rather a model of governance that has largely been cast aside.[5] Brien Hallett makes a strong case that when it comes to the application of military force abroad, modern American presidents have become like "kings and emperors," with few restraints on their ability to wage war.[6]

President Obama's idea of a strong commander in chief is especially interesting given the national mood after his election to the presidency. Obama promised to give Americans a new hope in government and opportunity as well as a new future in a postpartisan world. On foreign policy, Obama promised that "a new dawn of American leadership is at hand" and that he would not fight wars of choice but rather only wars of necessity.[7] Yet now with one term completed and well into his second term, at least one element of Obama's presidency has remained remarkably similar to the presidencies of George W. Bush and all of his post–Second World War predecessors. When it comes to determining if and when the United States will use force abroad, the president, as Bush argued in his own presidency, remains "the decider." At the same time, Congress's senior leaders, largely in bipartisan fashion, have often actively worked to avoid their constitutional duty to check the commander in chief in substantive and legislative ways. Active deference to the commander in chief often best describes how Congress behaves when the United States mobilizes for combat abroad.

The need to study how the United States enters war remains as relevant as ever. During the Obama administration so far, the United States has expanded its military presence in Afghanistan and used new technology to increase its use of drone missile strikes across Pakistan, Yemen, and Somalia. The Obama administration has also faced new and unexpected piracy challenges on the Indian Ocean and engaged in a sustained, seven-month bombing operation in Libya. After his first term in office, Obama is a president who in many ways has utilized diplomacy and international organizations to advance peaceful solutions to international crises, but he has also remained willing to use both overt and covert military power to confront threats abroad and seek political outcomes.[8]

Analysis of the U.S. military is also necessary when considering the amount of financial resources devoted to the U.S. Department of Defense. In terms of absolute dollars spent, in 2011 the United States devoted more money to defense than the next thirteen top defense-spending countries combined, which includes all other permanent members of the UN Security Council (China, France, Russia, and the United Kingdom) as well as Brazil, Germany, and India. By some measures, the United States accounts for 41 percent of all military spending across the globe.[9] Thus, the case for ongoing study of U.S. foreign policy and the manner in which the United States decides to use its military seems as important as ever.

This book examines five cases of U.S. military action during Obama's presidency. In the process, two themes become evident. First, President Obama, much like his predecessor commanders in chief, has continued to protect what the executive branch views as its exclusive power: the power to determine if U.S. military force will be used abroad. Though this theme reveals itself in different ways, the pattern is clear in all cases.

A second theme advanced across the book is that Congress's abdication of its constitutional war powers to the president is the norm, which occurs regardless of the political party in power. Employing an argument advanced in previous research by Stephen R. Weissman, the book presents evidence indicating that Congress's leaders, regardless of political party, actively work to defer decision-making authority regarding the use of force to the president.[10] These findings run counter to some of the existing research on the practical application of war powers, which argues that, like other areas of U.S. foreign-policy making, political partisanship is alive and well and that commanders' in chief decisions are often strongly influenced by the opposing political party in power. As demonstrated here, however, partisan behavior exists indeed, but not to the extent that constitutional or meaningful limitations are placed on the commander in chief. Rather, congressional leaders, regardless of political affiliation, go to great lengths to avoid political and constitutional accountability for U.S.

military action abroad. These themes are even evident in the 2013 crisis involving Syria, when President Obama uncharacteristically turned to Congress to request its approval for military action. In this case, President Obama still protected the idea of a unilaterally empowered presidency, and nearly all Republican and Democratic congressional leaders actively deferred to the president.

Not all members of Congress have willingly forfeited their right to oversee and check the commander in chief. In 2011, as the Obama administration began its missile strikes on Libya, Congressman Dennis Kucinich (D–Ohio) noted, "We are in a constitutional crisis because we have an administration that has assumed for itself powers to wage war which are neither expressly defined nor implicit in the Constitution nor permitted under the War Powers Act. This is a challenge not just to the administration but to this Congress, itself."[11] Nonetheless, Kucinich's efforts and similar ones witnessed during the Obama presidency have often been blocked by Congress's senior leaders, who prefer that the president take all political and constitutional responsibility for the use of force abroad. This book seeks to provide in-depth case study analyses of the political process during the Obama presidency that has resulted in another nearly omnipotent commander in chief.

Organization of the Book

Chapter 1 provides the necessary background on war powers in the aftermath of the Second World War, which includes brief summaries of America's entry into the UN and the North Atlantic Treaty Organization (NATO), the Cold War environment that fostered the empowerment of the commander in chief, the War Powers Resolution (WPR) of 1973, and the political environment that Barack Obama inherited on becoming the commander in chief. This chapter also examines Barack Obama's and Joe Biden's views on war powers when they served in the U.S. Senate and argued that Congress has an important constitutional duty and right to check the president both before and during war. Unlike many members of Congress, Obama and Biden were expressly interested in constitutional war powers and made the case that the president's "monarchism" with respect to war practices went directly against the notion of checks and balances.[12] The chapters that follow assess the interplay between the

White House and Congress during President Obama's first term in cases where the United States either increased its military presence abroad in existing conflicts or introduced U.S. military forces into new conflicts or regions. The final chapter addresses the war powers interplay over Syria in 2013.

Chapter 2 examines President Obama's two troop surges in Afghanistan in 2009 as well as the increased use of drone missile strikes in Pakistan and Yemen. Though a strong case can be made that his military decisions met the constitutional standard for military conduct during war, this chapter also demonstrates the widespread deferential behavior from Congress toward the commander in chief and the virtual absence of a role for members of Congress—especially its leaders—in making these major military decisions for the United States.

Chapter 3 addresses the Obama administration's increased military presence in the Indian Ocean in counterpiracy operations. Despite Congress's constitutional power "to define and punish Piracies and Felonies committed on the high Seas" (Art. 1, sec. 8) and a variety of U.S. combat operations involving uses of force and the rescue of foreign nationals, this chapter demonstrates that Congress granted the commander in chief wide and essentially unlimited discretion in determining how military force will be used to address this security challenge. Few members of Congress expressed any substantive interest on the issue of piracy or the subsequent military operations used to thwart Somali pirates.

Chapter 4 turns to the U.S. military bombing campaign in Libya, which offers an especially illustrative test case of President Obama's views on constitutional war powers during his presidency. This chapter demonstrates that congressional leaders, most importantly Speaker of the House John Boehner (R–Ohio), played an instrumental role in fostering Congress's abdication of constitutional authority on the use of force. Moreover, this case highlights the novel arguments the Obama administration made to insulate itself from the requirements of the WPR while maintaining that the United States was not involved in "hostilities" in Libya.[13] In this respect, Obama helped expand presidential prerogatives and created new avenues for the president to avoid congressional applications of the WPR.

Chapter 5 turns to the Obama administration's decision to place U.S. Special Forces in Central Africa in an attempt to capture human rights abuser Joseph Kony and other leaders of the Lord's Resistance Army. Congress's role in this case is different in that although it played an active role in steering U.S. foreign policy, it also empowered the commander in chief to take military action. Much like other U.S. military actions abroad, in this case Congress utilized legislative tools simultaneously to defer military powers and to confer decision-making authority to the president.

Chapter 6 examines Congress's abdication of war powers by providing a comparative case study of John McCain's (R–Ariz.) and John Kerry's (D–Mass.) views on war powers over the course of their careers in the U.S. Senate. In doing so, this chapter looks at the leading roles that two senior senators played in structuring U.S. foreign policy and the use of force abroad, including Obama's military strikes in Libya. Given the heightened influence senior senators can have in shaping policy, especially in the area of foreign and security affairs, such a focus is merited for evaluating the application of Congress's war powers.[14] Though McCain and Kerry describe their views on the Constitution and the WPR much differently, the policy result of their statements and behaviors for the commander in chief has been the same—that is, an empowered president both before and during the use of force abroad.

The book concludes with a brief case study of the interplay between Congress and the president over Syria in 2013 and follows with a set of policy discussions and recommendations centered on rectifying this imbalance of war-making power as well as the policy implications of an empowered commander in chief.

Like other commanders in chief, President Obama continues to create red lines that suggest an independent military power that runs directly counter to the constitutional notion of checks and balances. In 2014, Obama created another "line" when he warned Russia that "there will be consequences if people step over the line" in the Ukraine.[15]

This power has been achieved not simply by a president's assertion of such powers but by Congress's as well as a Republican and Democratic leadership's avoidance of constitutional responsibility for U.S. military action abroad. A more deliberative decision-making process for war that embodies checks and balances, at the least, meets a more legitimate constitutional standard, and may also help the United States avoid wars that have such profound economic, strategic, and moral consequences.

1

The War Powers Framework for the Obama Presidency

We have been sliding for 70 years to a situation where Congress has nothing to do with the decision about whether to go to war or not, and the president is becoming an absolute monarch. And we must put a stop to that right now, if we don't want to become an empire instead of a Republic.

—Congressman Jerrold Nadler (D–N.Y.),
Cong. Rec. H4535–6 (June 24, 2011)

Our Founders understood that waging war is not something that should be taken lightly, which is why Article 1, Section 8 of the United States Constitution gives Congress—not the president—the authority to declare war. This was meant to be an important check on presidential power. The last thing the Founders wanted was an out-of-control executive branch engaging in unnecessary and unpopular wars without so much as a Congressional debate. . . . Unfortunately, that's exactly the situation we have today in Libya.

—Congressman Ron Paul (R–Tex.), "Why I'm Suing the Obama Administration over Libya," *Daily Caller,* June 16, 2011

President Barack Obama's military actions abroad have produced bipartisan concern. Such voices were especially loud when Obama engaged in military action in Libya in 2011; he maintained that the Constitution permitted him to use force under his authority without specific congressional approval. Many members of Congress, constitutional experts, and some journalists argued that Obama had abused his authority as commander in chief.[1] When bipartisan challenges were raised, including by those who argued that the WPR had been violated, Obama dismissively referred to his critics as making "noise about the process" and that "a lot of this fuss is politics."[2]

Many would contend that today the office of the president has grown far more powerful than intended by the nation's Founding Fathers. Certainly, the current practices of modern commanders in chief differ substantially from the principles created by America's constitutional framers with respect to the decision to use force abroad. The Constitution provides the president the power to act as the country's commander in chief, but this power is balanced by a long list of congressional powers that speak directly to the use of force abroad. These constitutional authorities include the powers to declare war, to provide for the common defense, to grant letters of marque and reprisals, to provide and maintain a navy, to suppress insurrections and repel invasions, and to raise and support armies (Art. I, sec. 8). When discussing these powers, especially the power to declare war, James Madison's notes on the 1787 Constitutional Convention make it clear that the constitutional framers believed that the president may use force unilaterally only to "repel sudden attacks." Otherwise, the use of force requires congressional approval.[3]

The history of the constitutional ratification debates is similarly clear. Analysts have identified many instances when the framers and their supporters confirmed the understanding reached at the Constitutional Convention: war could not be entered into solely through a decision from the executive branch; legislative approval was required; the commander in chief was not permitted to act in the same manner as the British monarch, who could take his country to war at will. Although some analysts and politicians, including former deputy assistant attorney general John Yoo and former senators Barry Goldwater (R–Ariz.) and John Tower (R–Tex.), make the case that the Founding Fathers wanted a truly empowered commander in chief who would not be constrained by the legislature in national-security affairs, the historical evidence is far more compelling that the framers feared a monarchical military leader and thus imposed meaningful checks on a president's independent decision-making authority for war.[4]

For much of the nineteenth century and through nearly half of the twentieth century, presidents tended to respect this basic understanding of checks and balances. In the years before the Second World War, many presidents considered Congress the ultimate decider in determining if and when force would be used. In many instances, presidents respected Congress's war powers and actively sought explicit legislative approval prior to the use of military force.[5]

Many analysts agree that with the onset of the Cold War Congress began the practice of deferring to presidential military ambitions by granting the commander in chief considerable leeway to defend the United States against perceived communist threats. At the same time, presidents began to make more expansive unilateral assertions of their war powers, such that Congress's war powers became much less meaningful in restraining U.S. commanders in chief.[6]

Some may contend that U.S. membership in the UN diminished Congress's constitutional role to check the commander in chief because the UN Security Council can take votes to authorize military action. Yet the legislative history surrounding U.S. membership in the UN is clear. In the United Nations Participation Act of 1945 and through the various committee hearings held prior to joining the UN, congressional leaders explicitly protected their constitutional war powers authority. The United States could not participate in UN-sanctioned military operations without explicit approval from Congress.[7]

Much the same evidence exists for U.S. membership in NATO. Though Article 5 of the Washington Treaty of 1949 calls on all NATO allies to come to the defense of a fellow member upon attack, such an attack is not an immediate and unquestioned trigger for military response from the allies.

The treaty was carefully written so as to respect the U.S. Congress's war authority, and the legislative deliberations regarding U.S. membership in NATO protected Congress's constitutional powers.[8] Nonetheless, American presidents have used UN and NATO endorsements, especially in the post–Cold War era, to make their case for unilateral presidential military authority, which Congress has accepted for the most part. A number of analysts highlight the Korean War in 1950 as a significant and transformative shift in executive–congressional relations, when President Harry Truman argued that a UN Security Council resolution permitted the United States to engage in military operations in Korea without congressional authorization. With the Cold War's onset and the widely shared belief in Congress and the American public that North Korea's communists represented a direct threat to the United States, most members of Congress avoided discussions of the United Nations Participation Act of 1945 and instead rallied around Truman's desire to use force unilaterally.[9]

One effort to rein in the commander in chief out of concern for abuse of presidential authority during the Vietnam War occurred with the passage of the War Powers Resolution in 1973. Among its requirements, the WPR called for the president to "consult" with Congress both prior to and during a military operation. It also required that the president gain congressional approval for a U.S. military operation lasting more than sixty days, with the possibility of an additional thirty-day extension in case of an emergency to get legislative approval. The president was also required to notify Congress in writing within forty-eight hours of the onset of military operations, which applied to all armed forces when engaged in "hostilities."[10]

Though the WPR was arguably well intentioned as an effort to control the commander in chief in future military operations, much research notes the deleterious effect it has had on Congress's war powers, which has led to the further empowerment of the commander in chief. Since its passage, all presidents have generally viewed the WPR as an unconstitutional infringement of their own perceived military powers.[11] In practice and in various efforts to circumvent the resolution, presidents have utilized expansive definitions of the term *consult* to avoid meaningful dialogue with Congress. Many major military operations, including President Ronald Reagan's use of force in Grenada in 1983 and President George H. W. Bush's invasion of Panama in 1989, fell well within the sixty-day time line. Moreover, presidents have often used semantics to insulate themselves from the language of the WPR by arguing that they were not truly engaged in "hostilities."[12] Recent presidents have even used force beyond the sixty-day limit, including President Bill Clinton, who conducted bombing operations in Kosovo in 1999 for seventy-eight days yet failed to implement the WPR's requirements. Thus, despite the range of constitutional and statutory powers Congress has available to check the commander in chief, presidential military power has grown considerably since the Second World War.

Even in the context of a presidency in which the chief executive faced an ostensibly assertive Republican Congress for the last six years of his presidency and in an environment in which the president did not have good political standing with the U.S. military and limited prior experience in foreign affairs, Bill Clinton was still able to make unilateral assertions of power as commander in chief, which Congress largely accepted.[13]

The administration of George W. Bush similarly made bold assertions of its alleged independent power to use force abroad. Although Congress specifically granted Bush broad military discretion for the global war on terror and later for the war in Iraq, many elements of the executive–congressional interplay at the time are illustrative of a commander in chief who accepted few restrictions on his perceived authority to use force abroad.[14] For example, in the lead-up to the war in Iraq, the Bush administration initially maintained that it would consult Congress before a war, but that it did not need congressional approval to use force against Saddam Hussein.[15] Upon considerable political pressure from Congress for Bush to request authorization, a vote to use force eventually occurred. Yet Congress's checking and oversight role in this case was nevertheless quite limited because Congress ceded to the president the actual decision on whether to use force at his own determination.[16]

Bush, like Bill Clinton in 1994, also made extensive claims as commander in chief in the U.S. deployment of troops to Haiti in late February 2004 as part of a UN peacekeeping operation. In this case, U.S. forces were deployed to protect Haiti's presidential palace and to help restore stability to a country that was rapidly unraveling, with insurgents using force against police forces and threatening to overthrow Haitian president Jean-Bertrand Aristide. Nonetheless, when U.S. forces were deployed, few members of Congress questioned the president on the decision to send these troops, and no legislative effort was made to challenge Bush's asserted authority to send American troops into a civil conflict where conditions were far from stable.[17]

One additional example of Congress's willingness to defer to President Bush's wishes was evident after the newly elected Democrats gained majority status in the House of Representatives and the Senate after the 2006 midterm elections. After campaigning nationally for an end to the U.S. military presence in Iraq and highlighting the faulty claims advanced by the Bush administration to justify the war, the Democratic-led Congress quickly succumbed to President Bush's new military plan to increase the U.S. military presence in Iraq through a 20,000-troop surge.

This deference, which was fostered by Congress's democratic leadership, contrasted directly with the Democrats' electoral promises. Certainly, a number of congressional Democrats expressed their concerns with Bush's 2007 troop surge,[18] yet the Out of Iraq Caucus still contained only one-third of House Democrats and few of the newly elected Democrats. Most newly elected Democrats rapidly became much more moderate in their criticism of President Bush upon taking their congressional seats. Though the caucus was vocal, it was able to do little to prevent the Democratic leadership and the Republican rank and file from supporting and financing President Bush's new plan to intensify the war in Iraq.[19]

The vast majority of past and current research on U.S. constitutional war powers maintains that presidents have often acted unilaterally with regard to their perceived powers as commander in chief and that since the Korean War Congress has largely deferred to presidential leadership on the decision of whether to use force abroad.[20] And as one considers the political environment in the immediate years preceding the Obama presidency, it seems evident that George W. Bush was able to make wide claims of military power and authority as Congress—both Republican and Democratic led—continued to support his military endeavors, even at times when public-opinion poll numbers were abysmally low for him.[21] A strong commander in chief triumphed over a compliant Congress even when the Congress was led by Democrats—Speaker of the House Nancy Pelosi (D–Calif.) and Senator Harry Reid (D–Nev.). It is in this context and political environment that Barack Obama and Joe Biden took their positions in the White House, which appeared ripe for a period of strong leadership as exercised by the commander in chief. That said, no president-elect or vice president–elect in the modern era had such extensive histories of supporting meaningful and substantive checks on the commander in chief prior to their leadership positions in the executive branch. Obama and Biden's records in the Senate certainly raised the possibility that an Obama/Biden White House would exercise power differently from their predecessors.[22] For these reasons, it is worthwhile to study their records in the Senate.

Senator Joe Biden and War Powers

Joe Biden was first elected to the U.S. Senate in 1972, where he remained until assuming the office of vice president in 2009. It is first notable that

Biden became vice president in an era when the office has gained new prominence in shaping both U.S. domestic and international policy. Since the vice presidency of Walter Mondale and through the vice presidency of Richard Cheney, this office has grown considerably in importance with increased responsibilities in the executive branch.[23] This was similarly true early in the Obama presidency as Biden was considered a close confidant of the president, who turned to him for advice, especially in the area of international affairs.[24] One of Biden's major areas of interest while serving for more than three decades in the U.S. Senate was U.S. foreign policy. At the time of his election as vice president, he was serving as the chairman of the Senate Foreign Relations Committee. For all of these reasons, it seems legitimate and relevant to the current presidency to understand Biden's previously expressed views on war powers and the constitutional authority to use force abroad.

Among U.S. senators, Joe Biden was especially well versed on constitutional war powers, which was evident through an array of speeches he gave on the Senate floor, his service on the Senate Foreign Relations Committee, his introduction of legislation aimed at limiting presidential military actions, and his published scholarship on this issue. Biden had a long record of advocating for congressional war powers and the notion that presidents may not use force without congressional approval. At the same time, however, he also argued that there are exceptions when the commander in chief may use force without congressional authorization, and he supported some unilateral military actions by presidents. He thus has an inconsistent record on this issue.

The most substantive legislative example of Biden's interest in war powers is evident in his proposed "Use of Force Act." This proposal stemmed from his participation on the Special Committee on War Powers, established in 1987 by the Senate Foreign Relations Committee partly in response to the Reagan administration's decision to place Kuwaiti oil tankers under the protection of the U.S. flag in 1987 without congressional consultation. More generally at the time, some members of Congress had grown increasingly concerned about the expansion of power exercised by the commander in chief and the WPR's perceived failures and limitations.[25]

In explaining much of the logic for his legislative proposal, Biden published a coauthored article on the topic in 1988 in the *Georgetown*

Law Journal, which demonstrated a detailed and historically grounded understanding of war powers, including a discussion of James Madison's *Notes of Debates in the Federal Convention of 1787,* where Madison summarized the Founders' belief that a commander in chief may use force independently only to "repel sudden attacks." Otherwise, Biden noted that congressional approval to use force is required.[26] In addition, Biden's article made references to early American presidents, who stated clearly that force could not be used without legislative approval. Moreover, it discussed two key U.S. Supreme Court cases, *Bas v. Tingy* (4 U.S. 37 [1800]) and *Talbot v. Seeman* (5 U.S. 1 [1801]), that built on the understanding that congressional approval is required for essentially the full gamut of U.S. military engagements. Biden and his coauthor also quoted President James Buchanan's view that "without the authority of Congress the President cannot fire a hostile gun in any case except to repel the attacks of an enemy."[27]

In this discussion of the history of war powers, Biden also established an understanding of other perspectives on war powers, including the view that a president may use force without congressional approval. He and his coauthor referred to these claims as the "monarchist" perspective, which evolved and emboldened the commander in chief after the Second World War as Congress retreated from exercising meaningful checks on the president in the face of communism. Biden's academic views square with the majority of scholars who have published on war powers and thus demonstrate considerable familiarity with major scholarly works on war powers, which is uncommon for a U.S. senator.

Many of these themes are evident in Biden's proposed Use of Force Act, in which he called for a joint decision framework such that the president is required to consult with Congress prior to and during the use of force abroad. Biden made the case that "joint deliberation" fosters U.S. national-security interests. In this proposal, however, he did address five military situations in which the commander in chief would be permitted to use force without congressional consultation or approval. These situations include the ability to repel an armed attack; the right to respond to a "foreign military threat that threatens the supreme national interest under the United States under emergency conditions" that does not permit time for congressional consultation; the ability to rescue citizens abroad from emergency situations; the ability to "forestall an imminent act of international terrorism" directed at the United States; and the ability to protect the rights of "innocent and free passage in the air and seas."[28]

Soon after the publication of his war powers article, Biden also suggested that the president may also use force as long as a UN Security Council resolution existed and Congress had been consulted.[29] Biden later included this exception in his 1992 Use of Force Act proposal,[30] but in the lead-up to the war resolution vote on the Gulf War in 1991, he argued that President Bush did not have authority to use force in Iraq, despite the Security Council's approval. He noted that "the choice to go to war remains with the Congress, and the Congress alone, as it always does."[31] The UN Security Council exception for the president did not appear in Biden's 1995 or 1998 proposals.[32]

In many respects, the situations that Biden discussed permit the president to use force quite liberally and allow substantial room for the commander in chief to interpret when and how to use force. In this regard, his proposal can be fairly criticized for granting substantial war powers to the commander in chief and thus further distancing the Congress from its constitutional duty to check the president. Biden's interest in allowing the commander in chief to use force with UN Security Council authorization but not congressional approval also contradicts the legislative history of U.S. membership in the UN.

At the same time, the core principle in Biden's proposal centered on a notion of shared presidential and congressional responsibility to determine when force may be used. According to the proposal, most of the situations in which the president is permitted to act without congressional approval involve "emergency" conditions. Without an emergency, congressional consultation is required, although the proposal did not specifically require congressional approval. In order to foster such consultation and to require meaningful dialogue between the congress and commander in chief, Biden called for the creation of a "congressional leadership group" consisting of House and Senate leaders from both parties. This group would meet periodically to encourage sustained consultations between the commander in chief and key foreign-policy and intelligence officials in the executive branch.[33]

Although Biden's proposal is unquestionably open to criticism from those who argue for greater congressional involvement in use of force decisions, it is clear that it sought to move away from what he viewed as the commander in chief's "monarchist" practices and that it considered enhanced congressional involvement in military decisions both constitutional and useful in terms of political practice. In this respect, Biden seemed to recognize the value and appropriateness of congressional involvement in what he would likely view as "nonemergency" military situations; otherwise, he argued, presidents are not permitted to assert unilateral decision-making authority for warfare.

Apart from Biden's scholarly writings and his Use of Force Act proposal, over the course of his Senate career he took a number of positions on presidential military actions that provide additional insight regarding his views on the balance of war powers. In a number of military actions, he called for prior congressional input and approval before a commander in chief may use force. He was an early supporter of Senator Jacob Javits's (R–N.Y.) efforts to revise the war powers arrangement and was a co-sponsor of Javits's efforts in 1973 to encourage the Senate to take up what eventually became the WPR.[34] In the first term of Ronald Reagan's presidency, Biden was also quite clear in calling for the application of the WPR to the U.S. troop deployment to Lebanon. In doing so, Biden clearly expressed his support for a congressional role in determining whether troops should remain deployed abroad in this peacekeeping mission.[35] In referencing the specific language of the WPR, well before the suicide truck bombing that took 241 American lives in Lebanon, Biden noted that "when the marines were sent as part of the multinational force, I believe they were entering into an area of hostilities. Some disagreed with that assertion of mine back then in the Foreign Relations Committee, but I think they are hostilities. And I think the War Powers Act should have been triggered immediately and [I] have so stated in the past."[36]

Biden made a nearly identical argument in 1984 when debate arose in Congress over President Reagan's deployment of American troops to El Salvador. Biden was again clear in this case, noting that "the President does not have the authority to make war, he has the authority to conduct a war. A Commander in Chief does not initiate a war, he conducts a war." In the same speech, calling for congressional oversight of the commander in chief, he pleaded with the president to "let us be part of what is our constitutional obligation."[37]

But Biden had previously supported Reagan's troop deployment to Grenada in 1983, which occurred without congressional consultation and has largely been viewed as a unilateral U.S. troop deployment by the commander in chief. He noted that, based on the intelligence briefing he had received, the president was justified to act.[38]

Thus, across these three cases in the Reagan administration, Biden's record on war powers is mixed. At times, he quite forcefully advocated for Congress's war powers authority when other members of Congress said little on the issue, but on Reagan's military operation in Grenada he supported the commander in chief's unilateral action.[39] Biden also sought to invoke the WPR, whose critics note may empower the commander in chief, but he also referenced the WPR in an effort to rein in U.S. military deployments.

Biden's record in other presidential administrations is similar in its call for congressional checks on the commander in chief. Senator Biden argued against empowering George H. W. Bush militarily prior to the use of force in Panama in 1989.[40] In addition, he was clear in calling for meaningful legislative actions to limit Bush prior to Operation Desert Storm. In the lead-up to the 1991 Gulf War, while expressing his position and views on the limitations on the commander in chief, he referenced Founding Fathers James Madison, Elbridge Gerry, and Alexander Hamilton, who in his historical recollection were quite specific: "The real issue was authorization of war, which the framers did not intend to give to the President."[41] Biden openly challenged President Bush's opinion that the commander in chief was constitutionally permitted to use force against Saddam Hussein without congressional approval.[42]

When the Senate conducted its final debates over whether to support President Bush's desire to use force in Iraq in 1991, Biden spoke at length regarding his opposition to the view that a president can independently initiate military action, quite poignantly stating, "On this point the Constitution is as clear as it is plain. While article II of the Constitution gives the President the power to command our troops, article I of the Constitution commits to Congress—and Congress alone—the power to decide if this Nation will go to war. The Framers of our Constitution took great pains to ensure that the Government they established for us would differ from the rule of the British monarchs. They knew firsthand of the consequences of leaving the choice between war and peace to one man."[43] When the civil conflict in Bosnia erupted in 1992, Biden was quick to voice his support for military action to prevent additional atrocities in the Balkans, but he also called upon Congress to exercise its constitutional powers to authorize U.S. military action prior to engagement. Although the Congress was nearing an adjournment for the 1992 fall elections, Biden introduced a resolution that called upon the Senate to support military action if necessary but simultaneously encouraged the UN Security Council to authorize the creation of no-fly zones in Bosnia that would permit military enforcement of such zones. He noted, "I believe Congress should—as a matter of policy and as a matter of constitutional principle—act to provide such authority before adjournment."[44] In this case, Biden demonstrated his willingness to use force as well as his respect for Congress's role in making military decisions for the United States.

During the Clinton administration, Biden is remembered for being a strong advocate of U.S. and NATO military intervention in the Balkans and for his support of military strikes against Yugoslavian president Slobodan Milosevic.[45] At the same time, however, he argued that President Clinton "and the Presidents under whom I have served have all misread the Constitution" and made assertions as commander in chief that the constitutional framers had not intended. In the Clinton administration, Biden advocated for greater limitations on the commander in chief in the aftermath of the crisis in Somalia in 1993, in the lead-up to the U.S. troop deployment to Haiti in 1994, and through repeated proposals of his Use of Force Act.[46] In the hours prior to NATO's air strikes on Milosevic's forces in 1999, Biden led the floor debate in calling for the Senate's authorization of Clinton's requested action, noting after the vote's conclusion that "I do not think the President has the authority to use force in this nature without our approval."[47] Although Biden demonstrated a nonpartisan interest in protecting and asserting Congress's war powers, he did not actively oppose presidential military actions that were not authorized by Congress, and certainly with respect to Bosnia in 1995 and Kosovo in 1999 he quite actively backed the president's military actions.[48]

In the presidency of George W. Bush, Biden's record is again mixed. In the limited discussion that took place prior to Congress's vote to authorize President Bush's global war on terrorism after the September 11, 2001, terrorist strikes, Biden acknowledged that Congress had provided the president wide latitude to wage a military response against those involved in the terrorist strikes. Yet he also noted that Congress had actually checked the president by not extending him powers to "deter and preempt any future acts of terrorism against the United States," which the White House had originally requested in its discussions with the members of Congress. Although Congress granted President Bush extremely wide authority to use force, which Biden supported, Biden still referenced the constitutional limitations placed on the president and his opposition to "extend these authorities"—that is, those proposed by the White House. Biden's statements are notable given how few others even raised the issue of Congress's constitutional checking role during this crisis.[49]

On the resolution to grant President Bush authority to use force in 2002 against Iraq, Biden's focus was primarily on stating that he did not support a doctrine of military preemption. His record on this vote reveals contradictions regarding his views on war powers at this time. Biden voted for one of Senator Robert Byrd's (D–W.V.) amendments that called for more deliberation and opposition to Bush's foreign-policy direction regarding Iraq. This amendment limited to one year the authorization to use force, but it failed in the Senate. In making his arguments for supporting the amendment, Biden noted that during war Congress's power of the purse is difficult to invoke against the president, and thus Byrd's proposal was useful in limiting the president's military powers. Biden was one of thirty-one senators who voted for this resolution.[50] In this respect, he voted to permit a congressional checking role and more generally was part of the deliberative political process that determined the merits of President Bush's movement toward war.

Biden, however, did not support Senator Carl Levin's (D–Mich.) amendment to require the president to return to Congress for permission to use force after he sought UN Security Council approval for military action. He argued that it was sufficient to grant the commander in chief discretion at that time to use force if necessary, whether UN Security Council authorization was gained or not.[51] Moreover, in the key and final vote on the authorization to use force, Biden voted with seventy-six other senators to grant the president wide authority to determine if military force against Saddam Hussein was merited.[52] His support for this resolution contrasts with his long-standing rhetoric in favor of *Congress's* role in determining if military action is an appropriate policy step.

But then, in another about-face, Biden took a much stronger stand on Congress's war powers and even impeachment authority when some commentators posed questions over a possible use of force against Iran in

2007. When interviewed by Chris Matthews at NBC that year, he was adamant in expressing his support for congressional war powers:

> MATTHEWS: You said that if the president of the United States had launched an attack on Iran without congressional approval, that would have been an impeachable offense.
> BIDEN: Absolutely.
> MATTHEWS: Do you want to review that comment you made? Well, how do you stand on that now? Do you think . . .
> BIDEN: Yes, I do. I want to stand by that comment I made. The reason I made the comment was as a warning. The reason I made—I don't say those things lightly, Chris. You've known me for a long time. I was chairman of the Judiciary Committee for 17 years, or its ranking member. I teach separation of powers and constitutional law. This is something I know.
>
> So I got together and brought a group of constitutional scholars together to write a piece that I'm going to deliver to the whole United States Senate, pointing out the president has no constitutional authority to take this nation to war against a country of 70 million people, unless we're attacked or unless there is proof that we are about to be attacked. And if he does—if he does—I would move to impeach him. The House obviously has to do that, but I would lead an effort to impeach him.[53]

In sum, Biden's Senate record on war powers is mixed. Although it is clear that in many instances he advocated for Congress's war powers, the constitutional framers' belief in checks and balances on the commander in chief, and "joint deliberation" between the president and Congress prior to the use of force, he also supported commanders in chief when they used force without congressional authorization. His support for Reagan's actions in Grenada, his backing of the Clinton administration's strikes in Bosnia and Kosovo, and his interest in supporting a commander in chief who had gained UN Security Council approval without congressional approval demonstrate an inconsistent record. His proposed Use of Force Act also invites the same kinds of problems faced by the WPR in that with it presidents can use the same semantic distinctions to avoid congressional oversight and limitations on the commander in chief.[54] What is clear, however, is that, unlike many members of the modern Congress, Biden demonstrated a well-grounded historical knowledge of war powers and on a number of occasions sought legislative remedies to a "monarchist" presidency that alone determines if force will be used abroad, a knowledge that is especially evident in his 2007 comments regarding a possible military strike on Iran. Some members of Congress favor a very strong, if not unlimited, commander in chief, and seem numb to the idea that Congress should check the president.[55] Senator Biden, in contrast, often demonstrated a commitment to checking presidential war powers.

Senator and President-Elect Barack Obama and War Powers

In contrast to Joe Biden's history on war powers, Barack Obama's Senate record on this subject is less extensive. It is clear, however, that on the few occasions when Senator Obama spoke about war powers, he believed that Congress was required to play an important checking role. He made clear that unless the country's self-defense were in question, as James Madison argued at the Constitutional Convention, a commander in chief cannot engage in military action without congressional approval.

After his successful 2004 campaign bid to become the junior senator from Illinois, Obama did not speak often about the appropriate constitutional balance of powers between the Congress and the commander in chief or in a substantive manner about his preferred strategy for Iraq.[56] His views on President Bush's policies toward Iraq and war powers, however, developed more clearly in late 2006 and early 2007 when Bush proposed and eventually implemented his troop-surge strategy.

The first major signs of Obama's willingness to challenge the commander in chief came in November 2006, when from the campaign trail he called for a new strategic direction for Iraq, maintaining that "Congress has given the Administration unprecedented flexibility in determining how to spend more than 20 billion dollars in Iraq. . . . This must end in the next session of Congress, when we assert our authority to oversee the management of this war."[57] In this case, Obama's views indicated a belief that Congress can influence *how* a war is waged, which certainly goes beyond the notion that Congress can check the president only prior to the initiation of warfare. Obama here showed a willingness to check the president on the actual conduct of a war.

With new Democratic majorities in the House and Senate in 2007 after the 2006 midterm elections, Obama elaborated on his views regarding Congress's ability to manage the war in Iraq and in particular regarding what he viewed as Congress's legitimate role to prevent additional troops from being deployed without congressional approval. As Bush's 20,000-troop-surge plan became evident, Obama noted, "It now falls on Congress to find a way to support our troops in the field while still preventing the President from multiplying his previous mistakes."[58] Expanding on these remarks, he commented, "I said publicly that it is my preference not to micromanage the Commander-in-Chief in the prosecution of war. Ultimately, I do not believe that it is the ideal role for Congress to play. But at a certain point, we have to draw a line."[59]

Senator Obama was later equally explicit about Congress's role in shaping U.S. war decisions when he proposed major troop reductions to Iraq and expressed his opposition to Bush's troop-surge proposals. For example, in arguing that President Bush had failed in Iraq, he argued, "That is why Congress now has the duty to prevent even more mistakes." In this same address, he added that under his troop-reduction proposal Bush would not be permitted to deploy additional troops to Iraq "without explicit authorization by the Congress."[60] Both comments clearly suggest meaningful ways in which Congress can influence war and provide a check on the commander in chief on both *how* a war is waged and *whether* more troops can be introduced into warfare. When Obama was queried on the constitutionality of his proposals, he responded that Congress's 2002 authorization to use force in Iraq did not permit President Bush total and absolute discretion in determining war policies. He remarked, "The notion that as a consequence of that authorization, the president can continue down a failed path without any constraints from Congress whatsoever is wrong and is not warranted by our Constitution."[61]

Perhaps Obama's clearest expression on Congress's constitutional war powers and the commander in chief came in an interview by the *Boston Globe* in 2007. Responding to a question related to the president's legal authority to conduct a bombing operation against Iran in the absence of congressional approval, Obama commented unambiguously:

The President does not have power under the Constitution to unilaterally authorize a military attack in a situation that does not involve stopping an actual or imminent threat to the nation. As Commander-in-Chief, the President does have a duty to protect and defend the United States. In instances of self-defense, the President would be within his constitutional authority to act before advising Congress or seeking its consent. History has shown us time and again, however, that military action is most successful when it is authorized and supported by the Legislative branch. It is always preferable to have the informed consent of Congress prior to any military action.[62]

Obama also noted that he had sponsored a Senate resolution that would forbid an "offensive" military action by the president against Iran.[63] These views are quite clear and reflect a view of the Constitution that closely squares with the Founding Fathers' intent.

As president-elect, Obama took one additional step that perhaps suggested some interest in protecting Congress's constitutional war powers. On December 12, 2008, he met with former secretaries of state James A. Baker and Warren Christopher, the two leading voices of the 2008 National Commission on War Powers, ostensibly to discuss their proposal to provide for greater restraints on the commander in chief's ability to wage war and for enhanced congressional input prior to the use of force. At the meeting's conclusion, Obama made no public statement, but his spokesman, Denis McDonough, who in the first Obama administration would serve as the director for strategic communications for the National Security Council, noted, "President-elect Obama expressed his appreciation for their work and said he would review the commission's proposal. . . . The president-elect underscored his commitment to working closely with Congress with bipartisan participation."[64] Although McDonough was clearly noncommittal, the decision to grant a meeting with Christopher and Warren suggested some willingness on Obama's part at least to discuss the proposal, which at its core (Baker and Christopher contended) was intended to share the decision to use force abroad more equally between Congress and the commander in chief.[65]

In their time as U.S. senators, Joe Biden and Barack Obama had extensive records of advocating for Congress's war powers. Among U.S. senators over the past three decades, Joe Biden is unique in his frequent calls for war powers reforms, his historical knowledge of war powers, and his nonpartisan calls for enhanced checks on "monarchical" commanders in chief. At the same time, he also supported unilateral actions by the commander in chief. Obama's record on this issue is more limited given his much shorter tenure in the Senate, but it nonetheless indicates a history of favoring congressional actions that can restrict a commander in chief both prior to the use of force and during a military operation. These views of the Constitution contrast sharply with those of all presidents since the Second World War, who have generally invoked unilateral claims to authorize force in their position as commander in chief. In many respects, Biden's and Obama's views in the Senate were different from those of previous commanders in chief and indicate a more balanced constitutional perspective that permits checks and balances on the commander in chief.

However, upon entering the White House, President Obama inherited the legacy of the George W. Bush administration and his predecessors, who essentially claimed unilateral war powers for the commander in chief. Despite the Constitution's clear limits on the president's initiation of military action abroad and the legislative histories of U.S. membership in the UN and NATO, presidents since the Second World War have asserted wide authority as commanders in chief. Moreover, since the WPR was passed in 1973, all presidents have also argued that it is unconstitutional and therefore does not restrict the commander in chief's military actions. This context certainly provides a compelling environment for a new president to simply follow suit and similarly assert broad military and war-making powers.

2

Afghanistan, Drone Warfare, and the Kill List

He's a president who is quite comfortable with the use of force on behalf of the United States.
> —Tom Donilon, President Obama's first national
> security advisor, quoted in Jo Becker and Scott Shane,
> "Secret 'Kill List' Proves a Test of Obama's Principles
> and Will," *New York Times*, May 29, 2012

It was clear from early in his administration that President Obama would approach Afghanistan differently from his predecessor. Bush's war in Afghanistan, which had commenced on October 7, 2001, after the terrorist strikes on September 11, produced considerable debate during the 2008 presidential campaign. Presidential candidate Obama frequently made the case that Bush had been distracted by the war in Iraq and consequently had not done enough to fight terrorism at its core, which Obama argued was in Afghanistan. Obama promised that as president he would more directly confront the Taliban and al-Qaeda in the region, an approach that became evident almost immediately in his presidency. What has become more of a surprise, however, is President Obama's vigorous embrace of drone warfare in this fight and in some respects his willingness to employ a form of Bush's doctrine of preemptive military force as commander in chief through the use of drone technology.[1]

This chapter examines two facets of Obama's military choices in

Afghanistan, the two troop surges in Afghanistan in 2009 and the evolution of his drone-strike policies carried out in Afghanistan, Pakistan, Yemen, and Somalia. In doing so, the chapter focuses on how President Obama interacted with Congress over these aspects of his foreign- and military-policy decision-making process. Although a good case can be made that Obama's military actions have legal basis and that Congress already authorized the commander in chief (during the George W. Bush administration) to take these steps, when considering the political challenges evident in Afghanistan and the significant increase of drone strikes, one might have anticipated enhanced congressional scrutiny of these policies. Moreover, as demonstrated in the previous chapter, Barack Obama and Joe Biden entered the White House with robust and sustained records in support of Congress's war powers and oversight authorities, including when the United States was already engaged in war. The evidence presented here, however, suggests that Congress played a minimal role in shaping Obama's military decisions for the United States. This war powers interplay followed the patterns evident in previous U.S. military operations, in which the commander in chief led and the Congress followed. Moreover, as Stephen Weissman's previous research suggests, senior members of Congress granted and encouraged tremendous discretion to the executive branch for these decisions.[2]

The Troop Surges in Afghanistan

Within weeks of his inauguration, Obama announced on February 17, 2009, his plans to send a marine expeditionary brigade and an army Stryker Brigade to Afghanistan at the request of Secretary of Defense Robert Gates and General David McKiernan, the commanding officer in Afghanistan.[3] This decision was reached without any notable public debate in Congress.

Approximately one month later Obama announced his plans to significantly revise the U.S. war strategy in Afghanistan, which included his plans to deploy 17,000 additional American combat forces and 4,000 military advisors to Afghanistan. In announcing his plans, Obama noted the existing bipartisan support for his current efforts and called upon Congress to approve a bill sponsored by Senators John Kerry (D–Mass.) and Richard Lugar (R–Ind.) to authorize a $1.5 billion military spending increase each year for five consecutive years to Pakistan, which had agreed to assist the United States in this broader military effort in Afghanistan. He also noted his support for a bill proposed by Senator Maria Cantwell (D–Wash.) and Representatives Chris Van Hollen (D–Md.) and Peter Hoekstra (R–Mich.) to provide additional economic assistance to Afghanistan.[4] The extent to which these members influenced President Obama and his senior advisors, if at all, is not clear, but at minimum the bill indicated that some members of Congress were in synch with the administration's efforts from the start.

In the aftermath of this proposal, Obama received what he sought. The House approved his request in a 368–60 vote, with 51 Democrats voting against the proposal. The Senate unanimously approved of the Kerry–Lugar proposal.[5] Although a small minority of House Democrats raised concerns regarding Obama's plans, even the most vocal antiwar critics of the Bush administration found it difficult to generate similar levels of criticism for President Obama. The Out of Iraq Caucus, the most assertive group of congressional critics of George W. Bush's war policies, did not transfer its criticism to Obama and his new war strategy in Afghanistan with the same intensity and by some accounts was "largely silent" on Obama's Afghan troop increase.[6]

Obama did not notify members of Congress of his administration's new military approach to Afghanistan in a letter to congressional leaders, though he did send a letter in June 2009 regarding all American combat-deployed troops to justify his administration's actions in Afghanistan and all other combat operations through his powers "pursuant to my constitutional authority to conduct the foreign relations of the United States and as Commander in Chief and Chief Executive," which is the same language his most recent predecessors had used regarding their own authorizations of U.S. military conduct abroad.[7] Given that the authorization to use force in Afghanistan passed by Congress on September 15, 2001, was so broad, a strong case can be made that in his troop decision Obama acted within his constitutional authority as commander in chief, and in that respect large-scale congressional involvement may not necessarily have been expected. The key part of the resolution that authorized military action in 2001 says that "the President is authorized to use all necessary and appropriate force against those nations, organizations, or persons he determines planned, authorized, committed, or aided the terrorist attacks that occurred on September 11, 2001, or harbored such organizations or persons, in order to prevent any future acts of international terrorism against the United States by such nations, organizations or persons."[8] Many would argue that with such an expansive authorization the commander in chief would unquestionably be permitted to increase the troop number in Afghanistan.

At the same time, at the onset of the Obama administration many analysts concluded that the mission in Afghanistan was failing.[9] When President George W. Bush was implementing the troop surge in Iraq in 2007, Senator Obama had called for a congressional authorization vote to allow Bush to move forward with this plan. Using this same logic, the Obama administration could have requested congressional authorization for the Afghanistan troop-surge decision before moving forward. Like President Bush, however, President Obama did not do so. The ground conditions in Iraq and Afghanistan were clearly different, and the specific authorizations for the uses of force in Afghanistan and Iraq were also different—with the war in Afghanistan being much broader in scope. In both cases, however, thousands of troops were added to combat missions that were widely viewed as failures and thus fell within the parameters that Senator Obama previously utilized when challenging President Bush. Nonetheless, Obama's decision to place 21,000 more American troops in Afghanistan received little legislative criticism and virtually no open debate in either the House or the Senate. It was, in essence, a fait accompli by midsummer 2009.[10]

Obama's second troop-surge decision entailed the deployment of 30,000 additional American troops as well as 7,000 additional troops from U.S. allies in NATO. By midspring 2010, nearly 90,000 troops from forty-five countries were contributing to NATO's International Security Assistance Force in Afghanistan, of which approximately 39,000 were not American troops.[11] Obama announced the new policy after nine "war council" meetings and extensive public lobbying by General McKiernan's successor, General Stanley McChrystal. Yet again the troop-surge decision was made with limited congressional involvement and nowhere near what Vice President Biden had portrayed in the past as "joint deliberation" between the branches. Although it is clear that Senator John Kerry played an important diplomatic role for the Obama administration after the flawed 2009 Afghan national elections and encouraged a reevaluation of U.S. military policy in the region, journalistic accounts of key deci-sion moments during the entire war council evaluation period indicate that "the White House spent little time courting Congress" and that "no overtures were made to party leaders."[12] White House chief of staff Rahm Emanuel was in close contact with Senator Lindsey Graham (R–S.C.), who was generally advocating for more troops, but members of Congress were otherwise not included in Obama's key war council debates over how to handle Afghanistan.[13]

For the remainder of Obama's first term, Congress generally remained supportive of the military operation. Other than the effort led by Con-gressman Dennis Kucinich (D–Ohio) in March 2010 that called for the withdrawal of American troops from Afghanistan but gathered yes votes from only fifty House Democrats and five Republicans, most members of Congress rallied behind Obama's heightened war efforts, with only a few House Democrats raising objections to the heightened military opera-tion.[14] A similar effort by Kucinich in 2011 received equally limited sup-port. Certainly, many members of Congress expressed frustration with the lack of progress in training Afghanistan's military forces as well as with the rampant corruption associated with Afghan president Hamid Karzai and his government, but by 2012 Afghanistan had moved off of Congress's political radar; few members discussed it in their political cam-paigns, and even the presidential candidates devoted little time to the issue.[15]

Drone Missile Strikes

Alongside President Obama's two major troop surges in 2009, another major strategic policy change was evident in Obama's increased willing-ness to use drone missile strikes on the Taliban and elements of al-Qaeda. Obama's strikes have been far more extensive than Bush's were, as is evi-dent in the figures given in tables 1 and 2. With the exception of 2008, when Bush struck Pakistani targets on thirty-five occasions, the use of drones was an otherwise infrequent occurrence during his presidency. However, upon entering office in 2009, Obama almost doubled the num-ber of drone strikes in Pakistan and then significantly increased the num-ber of strikes in 2010. Similarly, he began to strike aggressively in Yemen, as demonstrated in table 2, an increase culminating in forty-two strikes in

Table 1. Drone Missile Strikes in Pakistan*

Year	2004	2005	2006	2007	2008	2009	2010	2011	2012	2013
Strikes	1	1	3	5	35	53	117	64	46	28

Table 2. Drone Missile Strikes in Yemen*

Year	2002	2009	2010	2011	2012	2013
Strikes	1	2	4	10	42	26

Table 3. Total Number of Drone Missile Strikes*

Presidency	Total Number of Strikes
Bush in Pakistan	45
Obama in Pakistan (first term)	280
Bush in Yemen	1
Obama in Yemen (first term)	58

* Data on number of missile strikes are available in the *Long War Journal* at http://www.longwarjournal .org/pakistan-strikes.php. Others who measure the number of drone strikes include the New American Foundation at http://natsec.newamerica.net/drones/pakistan/analysis. The latter's numbers are very similar to the *Long War Journal*'s measurements, though occasionally slightly higher.

2012, compared to one strike in Yemen across the entirety of Bush's presidency. Obama also carried out drone strikes in Somalia. By the end of his first term, he had conducted more than six times the number of strikes than Bush had in both of his terms (table 3).

The Obama Administration and Drones

In an examination of the political and constitutional issues surrounding Obama's drone strikes, at least two themes are evident. First, a number of journalistic reports have made it clear that within the Obama administration the legality of drone strikes has received considerable debate. Second, although the various parts of the executive branch, including the Departments of Defense and State as well as the Central Intelligence Agency (CIA), have interacted and debated among themselves over drone strikes, Congress played a very limited checking role on the use of drones in Obama's first term.

Over the course of Obama's first term, a number of key developments took place within the administration over the drone strategy, most of which were highlighted by investigative journalists. Early in the Obama administration, senior officials felt confident that the 2001 Authorization for Use of Military Force passed after September 11 (Public Law 107-40, Senate Joint Resolution 23) continued to provide the administration with full authority to use drones. Yet as the use of drones progressed, Obama requested that Harold Koh, legal advisor to the State Department, develop an internal legal rationale for that use. In going public to make the legal case, in a March 25, 2010, speech before the American Society of International Law, Koh defended the use of drones, noting that Congress had authorized broad military action after September 11. He noted, however, the Obama administration's compliance with recognized principles of international laws of war, which emphasize the right to self-defense and a targeting strategy that seeks to kill as few civilians as possible.[16] Koh's views produced considerable debate from international legal experts but very little response from Congress.[17]

In 2011, more information came forward indicating that there had been additional debate in the White House in 2010 over whether the United States could kill an American citizen abroad who was collaborating with al-Qaeda. After a number of executive office agencies and departments were consulted, the result was a fifty-page document authored from within the Justice Department's Office of Legal Counsel outlining the case for the killing of an American citizen abroad. This memo, which has not yet been publicly released, helped outline the case for killing Anwar al-Awlaki, an American citizen who was collaborating with al-Qaeda, on September 30, 2011, in a drone Hellfire missile strike in Yemen as well as another American citizen, Samir Khan.[18] Al-Awlaki was a Muslim cleric who had actively recruited individuals to join al-Qaeda and had openly supported terrorist strikes against the United States.[19] For the purpose of this study, what is critical here is that the White House was undergoing much deliberation on the legality of such a strike, which suggests the legal and constitutional ambiguity of the commander in chief's actions.

Additional journalistic evidence published in 2011 highlighted a tremendous debate between the CIA, which sought greater leeway for the use of drones, and the Departments of Defense and State, which wanted greater control over the use of drones. Some of the fiercest critics of aggressive drone strikes were State Department employees located in Pakistan, who were able to convince senior Obama officials to place greater restrictions in their targeting selections.[20] However, journalistic reports in 2012 indicated that the Obama administration had expanded its targeting strategy to reach a broader range of al-Qaeda affiliates in Yemen. These reports again suggest significant debate within the administration regarding who could be struck.[21] Interagency discord over this military tactic was frequent across Obama's first term.

New York Times reporters published one of the more fascinating reports on drones and the Obama administration in 2012, revealing the presence of a "kill list." The list included the names of the individuals who were deemed worthy of direct military action and targeting. The report indicated that the target-selection process involved more than one hundred individuals in investigating and eventually proposing targets for consideration, which often demanded robust challenges and debate. This list would eventually reach President Obama and his senior advisors, who in close consultation with John Brennan, then deputy national security advisor for Homeland Security and Counterterrorism, made the final decision on whether to strike a target or not. Obama was involved in the approval process for every strike in Yemen and Somalia as well as for the most controversial targets in Pakistan, all of which entailed approximately one-third of all strikes. Apart from evaluating the intelligence presented regarding the targets, these strike decisions entailed consideration of the number of potential civilian casualties.[22] Thus, the White House had in place a rather deliberative process for managing the use of drones, which at times involved significant debate.[23]

On April 30, 2012, Brennan, like Harold Koh, also provided a public defense for the use of drones. He similarly made the case that the Authorization for Use of Military Force after September 11 provided the legal justification for the use of drones and that "the Constitution empowers the president to protect the nation from any imminent threat of attack." He noted the "rigorous standards" that the Obama administration used in selecting targets as well as the administration's compliance with international law and its respect for foreign states' national sovereignty.[24] President Obama himself said very little specifically about the use of drones, although when he did comment on them in 2012, he focused on the internal restraints that exist, noting that the use of drones was "kept on a very tight leash" and that he was authorizing only "pinpoint" strikes.[25]

Congressional Oversight?

If one accepts the Obama administration's claims at its word, that its use of drones has been directed solely at al-Qaeda and elements of the Taliban, such a use of force likely falls under the 2001 Authorization for Use of Military Force, as both Brennan and Koh maintained. Moreover, as noted earlier, all administration officials, including President Obama, made the case that great care went into the selection of all drone targets and that the Constitution empowers the president to direct U.S. war efforts. All of these supporting points suggest that one would expect limited input from Congress and that the commander in chief should control this facet of U.S. foreign policy.

Yet over the course of Obama's first term public scrutiny of drone strikes grew considerably as the number of strikes increased. By October 2012, it was clear that the UN was moving toward the creation of a special committee devoted to monitoring drone strikes, with special emphasis devoted to determining how many civilian casualties had resulted from these actions.[26] In the same year, the Pakistani Foreign Ministry also became increasingly critical of the use of drones, arguing that it was "illegal," an argument that was leading to an increasingly contentious diplomatic relationship between Pakistan and all of the NATO allies.[27] Some international legal experts also raised concern over the use of drones. Thus, given the broader public and international concerns raised over their use, one might think that congressional oversight would have been considerable. A review of Congress's attention to drones shows, however, that the record is mixed, but a strong case exists for a rather compliant Congress, with congressional leaders in bipartisan fashion supporting the commander in chief.

What is unique about Congress's oversight of drone actions is that the Obama administration's reporting protocol depends on who launches the drone. Micah Zenko notes that if the drone is fired by the Department of Defense, which normally means that the strike has been carried out by the Joint Special Operations Command, individual strikes are not reported directly to Congress's Armed Services Committees but in some capacity are addressed in a "special access" biannual report to Congress. If a drone is used by the CIA, however, the House Permanent Select Committee on Intelligence and Senate Select Intelligence Committee staffs are notified on a monthly basis.[28]

The public's knowledge of this oversight came in part as a result of journalistic criticism over the perceived lack of congressional oversight of Obama's drone program.

In response to a challenge from the *Los Angeles Times* in 2012, Senator Dianne Feinstein (D–Calif.), chairperson of the Senate Select Committee on Intelligence, noted that her committee staff had been briefed in twenty-eight different meetings to "review the strike records and question every aspect of the program including legality, effectiveness, precision, foreign policy implications and the care taken to minimize noncombatant casualties. . . . I have insisted on this oversight, and the committee has been satisfied with the results."[29] It later became clear that on a monthly basis House and Senate Intelligence Committee staff members had visited CIA headquarters, where they were informed of recent strikes with video images and might also have received sensitive intelligence information such as intercepted phone calls and other data that led to strike decisions. Mike Rogers (R–Mich.), chairman of the House Permanent Select Intelligence Committee, similarly argued that Congress had been informed on every drone strike up to that time and therefore was largely satisfied with the information provided by the Obama administration.[30] Some considered this level of oversight significantly improved compared to that for the Bush administration, although, as established earlier, the number of Bush-authorized drone strikes pale in comparison to Obama's.[31] In sum, it is clear that some measure of congressional oversight occurred and that leaders in the Senate and House felt that the Obama administration took appropriate steps to inform Congress about drone activity.

What is less clear from this evidence, however, is the degree to which senators and representatives participated in these briefings. Feinstein noted that "committee staff" attended the CIA briefings, as did further reports on this oversight. Committee staffers play important roles in helping members of Congress fulfill their representative roles, but at the same time they are not the ones elected to represent the constituents. It may also be to a congressperson's political advantage *not* to know the operational details on strikes, especially for strikes that result in civilian casualties. Thus, Feinstein's language suggests a degree of separation from genuine oversight, with members of Congress instead maintaining some distance in the actual oversight process.

Moreover, although it may be that secrecy on such matters is necessary for national-security interests, some analysts have noted the increasing frequency of private rather than public Intelligence Committee hearings. In 2012, the Senate Intelligence Committee held only one public hearing, a number that in effect limits the public's information on the war and restricts other members' access to information about the use of drones.[32]

One additional development in Congress's oversight of the drone program became evident when President Obama nominated John Brennan to serve as director of the CIA in 2013 after Obama's reelection. Then, Senator Feinstein's story changed considerably, arguing that Obama administration was *failing* to provide adequate information on drone usage. In addition, when discussing the use of drones, she demonstrated fairly limited knowledge of the larger public debate regarding the number of civilian casualties associated with such strikes. Her fellow Intelligence Committee member Senator Ron Wyden (D–Ore.) also continued with his complaints and calls for greater oversight of drones' use. He maintained that the Obama administration was continuing to purposely keep Congress uninformed on drones.[33]

Apart from the oversight provided by Congress's Intelligence Committees, other congressional committees, including the House Foreign Affairs Committee and the Senate Foreign Relations Committee, exercised very limited oversight on the use of drones during Obama's first term. When three American citizens affiliated with al-Qaeda were killed by drone strikes in Yemen, Senate Judiciary Committee chair Patrick Leahy (D–Vt.) made a public request to the Obama administration for the legal justification advanced for these killings, though critics pointed to the gentle nature of his request.[34]

The most public oversight provided by Congress on drones arguably came from a subcommittee of the House Committee on Government Oversight and Government Reform. In two sets of hearings, this subcommittee heard arguments regarding the legality of drone usage in 2010, with most participants making the case that drone warfare was being conducted in a legal manner.[35] Otherwise, there is little evidence of any sustained interest in the use of drones by congressional committees—that is, until Brennan's nomination as CIA director in 2013.

In contrast, the most vocal critic in the U.S. Congress of Obama's use of drones and the member who most frequently called for meaningful congressional oversight of drones was Congressman Dennis Kucinich (who served in the House from January 1997 to January 2013). In 2012, Kucinich argued that "the administration's unrestricted use of drones has taken us into undeclared wars in Pakistan, Yemen, Somalia, Sudan, and who knows where else, destroying not only alleged militants, but making a direct hit on international law and the U.S. Constitution. . . . The Constitution requires Congress to weigh in and demand information and legal justification for drone strikes."[36] In the same year, Kucinich made a similar plea for congressional oversight: "We cannot pretend that United States policy—which often lacks congressional involvement—with drones flying over Yemen and Somalia and Pakistan and Afghanistan and innocents killed, that there's not going to be blow-back or a backlash."[37] On another occasion, Kucinich made the case that "the drone program has thus far been conducted with no oversight from Congress or any judicial body."[38]

Kucinich, however, went beyond making independent speeches on the House floor in his effort to increase congressional oversight. Teaming with Congressman Ron Paul (R–Tex.), another longtime advocate of congressional war powers, he asked the House Judiciary Committee to issue calls for additional legal information from Attorney General Eric Holder regarding all legal documents related to drone strikes on Americans abroad.[39] Kucinich and Paul were able to generate a Judiciary Committee hearing on aspects of this question. Moreover, within the committee, three members—John Conyers (D–Mich.), Jerrold Nadler (D–N.Y.), Bobby Scott (D–Va.)—had previously written to the Obama administration on a number of occasions to request additional legal clarification of the president's drone strike practices.[40] However, when considering the proposal, Judiciary Committee chairman Lamar Smith (R–Tex.) made the case that Congress's Intelligence Committees had been providing good oversight of the drone program and that such an inquiry was therefore unnecessary. In addition, Congressman Conyers maintained that Kucinich and Paul had not sufficiently consulted Judiciary Committee members on this issue, so he too was unwilling to support their request. Thus, in a theme that will become even more evident in the chapter on U.S. military action in Libya, the committee defeated Kucinich and Paul in a voice vote with backing from the committee's senior leaders, who did not see the need for more aggressive oversight at the time.[41]

In 2013, in the aftermath of John Brennan's nomination to serve as CIA director and with heightened domestic and foreign pressure to increase Congress's oversight of drone missile strikes, both Senate Intelligence Committee chair Dianne Feinstein and Senate Armed Services chair Carl Levin (D–Mich.) pushed the Obama administration to allow for expanded and more collaborative checking roles for Congress. The administration in 2014 refused to comply with these requests. Moreover, the Senate Intelligence Committee's ranking Republican, Saxby Chambliss (R–Ga.), argued for maintaining the current reporting practices followed by the Obama administration. Some House members also argued against Feinstein's and Levin's requests, noting that a similar committee collaboration in the House would be unwise, given the size of the House Armed Services Committee. In short, some felt that too many members of the House would now have greater access to information on the drone program.[42] Thus, though a degree of heightened congressional interest in drone oversight existed at the onset of Obama's second term, the reporting practices remained much the same through 2014.

President Obama and Vice President Joe Biden have maintained the practice of keeping military decision making within the White House, in contrast to their greater advocacy of congressional war powers when they served in the U.S. Senate. Congress played a tertiary role at best in defining the two major troop-surge decisions in Afghanistan for the United States and did not play a critical role in shaping these decisions for the United States. And it has played the same slight or nonexistent role for the use of drones. Congress has provided some, albeit limited, oversight of the Obama administration, though this oversight has been carried out primarily by congressional staffers. Senior leaders of both parties, including Dianne Feinstein and Mike Rogers, have been compliant with the administration, and when challenges have surfaced over the need for greater checks and balances, congressional leaders have worked to protect the administration, insulating themselves from Congressmen Kucinich and others who have sought greater oversight role. As is demonstrated in this chapter, most members of Congress, at least in public, are content to defer to the commander in chief. This deference has largely been bipartisan, though when opposition to the president has occurred, it has come primarily from Democrats, which challenges the notion of an institutionally partisan role for Congress on war powers.

A rebuttal to these arguments may be that Congress's deference to the president suggests active support for the commander in chief. Indeed, for many members of Congress, this may be the case. Silence may equal backing for the president's military actions. That said, many analysts argued that the war in Afghanistan was failing miserably in 2009 when the troop-surge decisions were being made, yet few members of Congress opposed the president. Moreover, many legal experts and foreign states as well as the UN have expressed concern over the use of drones, especially in 2012, yet few members of Congress have raised public concern over their use. Thus, although very real and legitimate policy concern has existed in the broader public, the Congress and its leaders have institutionally engaged in a very minor checking role and certainly have not provided substantive opposition to the president. Such actions suggest that a behavioral norm of deference may better explain why Congress has chosen to follow the commander in chief.

It may also be that some members of Congress express their concern with the president's military actions privately and in fact may be contacting President Obama and White House officials to express their opposition to U.S. policy in Afghanistan, Pakistan, and Yemen. Indeed, one would suspect that many legitimate concerns are raised in this fashion. Members of Congress might even privately threaten to take action against the president if military policy changes are not adopted. Unfortunately, such private actions are very difficult to assess. Moreover, private complaints also inherently suggest a degree of congressional deference, whether it is to the president, whom the member does not want to challenge publicly, or to congressional peers or perhaps leaders, whom a member also does not want to confront publicly. U.S. military policy on Afghanistan may bear the evidence of such private complaints, but the public record and the nonuse of the constitutional means established for checking a commander in chief indicate institutional compliance with President Obama for this war, with senior leaders actively working to protect the commander in chief's claims for keeping congressional interference to a level that the administration prefers.

3

Fighting Pirates on the Indian Ocean

Global security threats and challenges continue to evolve well beyond the imaginations of what many thought possible only a decade ago. The rapid increase in piracy off the coast of Somalia and deep into the Indian Ocean during the Obama administration's first term is one of these formerly unfathomable threats. In 2009, Somali pirates attacked 214 vessels and successfully hijacked 46. The numbers of attacks increased to 237 in 2011, though there was a slight decrease in successful hijackings. The number of attacks and successful hijackings decreased substantially in 2012 and 2013. The gravity of this newly arrived threat during the Obama administration, however, produced responses from NATO, the European Union, and the UN Security Council, indicative of this threat's global dimension.[1]

Early in his presidency, Obama maintained that piracy "constitutes an unusual and extraordinary threat to the national security and foreign policy of the United States."[2] This security challenge also resulted in a number of decisions by the UN Security Council authorizing the use of force against the pirates. These decisions, in concert with a more aggressive American response, resulted in a number of U.S. military actions involving the use of force, including attempted rescues of American and foreign national hostages, and sustained military policing operations in the Indian Ocean. One of these operations entailed a hostage-rescue effort on land. These developments represent a significant change in how American military personnel are being used abroad and raise important and new constitutional questions over the authority to use force.

The U.S. Constitution states that Congress shall "define and punish Piracies and Felonies Committed on the high Seas" (Art. 1, sec. 8). Although many might have guessed that this line in the Constitution would have little relevance in the twenty-first century, it is now clear that Somali pirates have gained unexpected prominence in U.S. foreign and security policy. In this context, the Constitution suggests an important regulatory role for the U.S. Congress and in no way implies that piracy is to be handled independently by the commander in chief. Moreover, given that the UN Security Council intervened in this issue with a Chapter VII use-of-force authorization, congressional oversight and authorization, according to the UN Participation Act of 1945, are required. However, this chapter makes the case that President Obama, as commander in chief, has dominated the decision-making process and strategy surrounding pirates, while Congress has largely avoided constitutional responsibility for U.S. military conduct in response to piracy. Though counterpiracy operations raise somewhat different constitutional questions for the president and Congress than raised by a more clearly defined conflict between two warring factions, Obama's antipiracy policies and actions have war powers relevance, given a sustained U.S. military presence on the Indian Ocean as well as a number of military operations that have entailed some degree of combat and use(s) of force. As witnessed in Obama's decision-making process for Afghanistan and certainly for the use of drones, the executive–legislative interplay in this matter generally follows the practice of legislative deference to the commander in chief. Some members of Congress do have an interest in piracy issues, and those who have spoken out have largely favored strong U.S. military action, but they have avoided the question of constitutional responsibility for the use of force. This avoidance stems in part from the influence exercised by Congress's senior party leaders.

Somali Pirates and the U.S. Military

One of President Obama's first uses of military force that had the potential for tremendous political unpredictability came in April 2009 when a Somali pirate captured an American ship, the *Maersk Alabama,* and took its captain, Richard Phillips, hostage. After a number of days of negotiations, and when the U.S. military maintained that Phillips's life was in jeopardy, three U.S. Navy SEALs simultaneously fired on three Somali pirates, killing them instantly and rescuing Phillips.[3]

This incident, however, was only the beginning of U.S. military efforts against the pirates. One year later, while the USS *Nicholas* was on patrol in the Indian Ocean, it came under fire from a pirate skiff. Returning fire, the *Nicholas* pursued and caught the skiff. American forces eventually went aboard and captured three pirates. The *Nicholas* then sunk the skiff and located the pirates' mother ship, where two more pirates were captured.[4] In 2010, the USS *Ashland* was similarly shot at by pirates and then returned fire with two rounds, resulting in an actual fire on board the pirate skiff. The pirates abandoned the skiff by jumping into the water, where U.S. military personnel then rescued them.[5]

American forces have also come to the rescue of foreign nationals being held hostage. In September 2010, two dozen U.S. marines boarded the German-owned ship *Magellan Star,* rescuing the crew and all of the hostages. Lieutenant Colonel Joseph R. Clearfield, the operation's commanding officer, noted that "it was a combination of speed and overwhelming force" that led to the successful operation.[6]

Another quite dramatic use of American military personnel against Somali pirates came in March 2011, when four U.S. Navy warships responded to a hostage situation in which four Americans were being held on a yacht. After four days of negotiations, a rocket-propelled grenade was fired from the yacht toward the USS *Sterett,* one of the U.S. warships in the vicinity. In response, U.S. Navy SEALs boarded the yacht, only to find all four hostages had been killed. During a search of the yacht, the SEALs killed two pirates, one by gunshot and another by knife.[7] In the same year, U.K. and U.S. naval vessels also helped reclaim a captured Italian cargo ship being held by pirates.[8]

The rescue of captured American aid worker Jessica Buchanan by a U.S. military operation in early 2012 received extensive media coverage. In this military operation, which also entailed the rescue of Buchanan's Danish colleague, twenty-four Navy SEALs landed by parachute near the Somali village of Galkayo and successfully freed the aid workers through the use of force, killing all nine of her captors.[9] In the same year, American military personnel boarded a Somali pirate vessel and in the process rescued and freed thirteen Iranian hostages.[10]

President Obama did not notify members of Congress that these military actions would be taken or report that they had occurred. One possible explanation for the absence of communication is that the administration viewed these actions as so far removed from any military action associated with the WPR as to not require reporting, although it is clear that American troops were equipped for combat, were engaged in hostilities, and on many occasions used deadly force to accomplish their mission.

In sum, there is no shortage of U.S. military operations in response to pirates. Although each of these military missions is unique in its circumstances, all of them occurred in the context of a sustained military commitment and policy for dealing with Somali pirates and their various activities. In this respect, it would be a mistake to refer to such operations as "ad hoc" or simply as responses to emergency situations. Rather, they should be viewed in the context of a coordinated and sustained military presence abroad, which has also entailed the rescue of foreign nationals from a number of foreign states, including Germany, Iran, and Italy.

In part, the U.S. government's willingness to respond to these pirating actions is shaped around the actions of a variety of international organizations. In January 2009, U.S. Naval Forces Central Command created Combined Task Force 151 in an effort to more effectively police the Gulf of Aden, which was seeing especially rampant piracy at the time and was also the route for approximately 11 percent of the world's oil shipments. Combined Task Force 151 works with partner states to patrol these waters and focuses exclusively on counterpiracy operations.[11] These operations occur within the context of UN Security Council resolutions, which in response to a request from Somalia's Transitional Federal Government in June 2008 authorized the use of "all necessary means to repress acts of piracy and armed robbery."[12] Beginning in 2008, NATO also commenced a small antipiracy operation; it works in conjunction with the European Union, which also manages its own antipiracy mission, Operation Atlanta, including naval, air, and troop contributions from nearly every member.[13] Thus, the international response to piracy grew significantly at the onset of the Obama administration, with a number of major military operations evident during this time. However, to understand the president's and Congress's views on pirates, we must first understand the historical background of U.S. military actions aimed at pirates, which shapes modern discussions of this issue.

Constitutional History of Antipiracy Operations

As indicated earlier, the U.S. Constitution states that Congress shall "define and punish Piracies and Felonies Committed on the high Seas," though the Founding Fathers spent virtually no time debating aspects of this congressional power. James Madison's notes on the Constitutional Convention provide little record of meaningful dialogue on piracy and the Founding Fathers' views of it; this issue was barely discussed in Philadelphia. The Federalist Papers similarly provide virtually no insight on piracy and the management of this threat.[14] However, historians have offered some perspectives on how Congress and presidents later interpreted this power in the context of America's first trials with pirates.

One early indicator of a constitutional perspective on piracy came from America's first secretary of state, Thomas Jefferson, who in 1790 was forced to deal with Barbary pirates. Jefferson noted that it was Congress's responsibility to determine how the United States should deal with the pirates, whether with warfare, the distribution of tributes, the payment of ransoms, or any other policy. Jefferson maintained that it was Congress that was to direct policy and the president who would implement congressional directives.[15]

Upon becoming president, however, Jefferson later sent U.S. naval forces to the Mediterranean in 1801 to protect U.S. shipping interests that were being attacked by pirates. Upon reaching the region, U.S. forces engaged in direct military action against the pirates. In the aftermath of this conflict, Jefferson returned to Congress to inform them of these developments and to seek its guidance on future interactions with pirates.[16] This particular exercise of presidential power has generated much debate from scholars. War powers expert Louis Fisher notes that on the day before Jefferson became president, Congress gave the president authority to create a "naval peace establishment" to patrol against piracy. In this regard, Congress clearly authorized the president to take military action against the pirates. Jefferson, however, focused on the difference between defensive and offensive military action and maintained that defensive military actions could be conducted without explicit congressional approval, but offensive actions clearly required congressional authorization.[17] Thus, when the navy eventually used force, Jefferson maintained that the actions were authorized.

Other historians maintain that in an assessment of Jefferson's actions the emphasis should be placed on the directives given to the U.S. Navy for when it arrived in the Mediterranean, which certainly provided it with some discretion in determining how force would be used against the pirates, implying that the Jefferson administration was more broadly defining its powers to authorize the navy to use force as necessary.[18] Regardless of the particular emphasis various historians place on this issue, what is clear is that Jefferson saw himself limited by the Constitution in fighting pirates, and so upon the use of force he returned to Congress for guidance and direction. The result was that the president and Congress had a formal exchange of views on this issue, resulting in explicit authorizations to use force in these particular circumstances.[19] Jefferson's successor, James Madison, similarly sought approval from Congress to use force against pirates.[20] Thus, what is clear according to the historical record is that meaningful dialogue existed between the branches over the use of force, and the presidents in this period did recognize some limitations on their authority as commander in chief.

Another instructive historical example is from the administration of President James Monroe, who had an extensive dialogue with Congress over the threat and management of piracy. In the early 1820s, Congress authorized and oversaw a number of antipiracy operations in the West Indies. Yet in an especially telling remark Monroe noted, "Whether those robbers should be pursued on land, the local authorities be made responsible for these atrocities, or any other measure be resorted to suppress them, is submitted to the consideration of the Congress."[21] On January 30, 1823, Congress made "permanent law" (Title 33, chap. 7) that the president could use public vessels to respond to piracy threats and actions. Today, the law regulating piracy reads as follows: "The President is authorized to employ so many of the public vessels as in his judgment the service may require, with suitable instructions to the commanders thereof, in protecting the merchant vessels of the United States and their crews from piratical aggressions and depredations." Congress has made revisions to this act since 1823, though little change exists in the language that permits the president to use public vessels to suppress piracy.[22]

Though there were a number of additional incidents involving the U.S. military in dealing with pirates after the Monroe administration, including uses of force in Sumatra in 1827, Ivory Coast in 1843, and near Hong Kong in 1855, the piracy threat was much reduced from the 1830s to the modern era. As Europe became more stable, American and British antipiracy cooperation increased, and as the incentives decreased for foreign states to sponsor piracy, this threat reduced dramatically.[23] In addition, the emergence of steamships, which were much faster and better armed than pirate ships, posed a significant challenge to pirates.[24] What remains clear, however, is that piracy as a threat to national-security interests was not dealt with unilaterally by the president alone but rather was evaluated and voted on by Congress, often on a case-by-case basis. Though Jefferson may have exceeded his authority as commander in chief in dealing with the Barbary pirates, he nonetheless returned to Congress for their oversight and authorization to use force, as did the presidents who followed him.

Modern legal advocates of a strong commander in chief may also argue that because Congress empowered the president in 1823 with the permanent authority to use force against pirates as needed, President Obama today does have authority to do so, especially given that Congress has amended and reiterated the original language that was made permanent in 1823 in Title 33, chapter 7. Yet at the same time, as the previous evidence suggests, U.S. constitutional history also indicates a clear understanding that Congress was intended to be intimately involved in use-of-force questions surrounding piracy. It seems illogical to maintain that a "permanent law" from 1823 forever forbids Congress from ever exercising its constitutional duty to "define and punish Piracies." In addition, the scope of modern antipiracy operations is difficult to compare to those conducted in 1823. Antipiracy operations today involve multiple service branches, air and sea operations, international partners, and rescue missions of foreign nationals, which certainly seems to go beyond the current language of Title 33, chapter 7.

Moreover, with respect to the role of pirates and the role of the U.S. Navy in the world, from the 1820s up until the 1880s presidents and members of Congress who adopted "antinaval" policy positions dominated the political discourse. Members of Congress and Presidents John Quincy Adams and Andrew Jackson actively promoted a very limited role for the U.S. Navy and were clearly skeptical about the potential virtues of a big navy, which in their view would ostensibly invite new national-security threats with potentially limited gain. In these years, Congress demonstrated its ability to shape U.S. naval policies and thus implicitly how the navy would be used abroad.[25] In sum, the history of congressional involvement in antipiracy operations and more generally in monitoring the role of the U.S. Navy is significant.

One additional legal aspect of modern piracy that needs to be recognized is that international law governing piracy is far from clear. In highlighting this problem, Peter Pham notes that America's closest allies in Europe have very different ideas on how to handle piracy on the Indian Ocean and, more specifically, what to do with pirates upon capture. Some allies have released pirates on land after their capture, whereas other allies wish to apply laws against them.[26] Clearly no consensus exists among America's closest allies, including its NATO partners, over how to respond to piracy.

In addition, it is also clear that the notion of individual rights has evolved considerably in the United States and Europe since 1823. Thus, a law governing military behavior toward pirates shaped around the dominant norms in 1823 is no longer inherently applicable to the modern world. Some may retort that piracy, much like terrorism, is by definition wrong and therefore automatically worthy of military response regardless of the context, yet such a view is rather simplistic and certainly does not square with the current legal practices and notions of modern rights utilized by the United States and its European allies today. Much remains unclear on how to handle and prosecute pirates and what rights they may have.[27]

In addition to Congress's historic role in regulating the navy and the modern legal complexities of dealing with piracy—especially when allies are partners in these operations—it is also not self-evident that Congress's empowerment of the president in 1823 to conduct counterpiracy operations applies to the rescue of foreign nationals, which has occurred on a number of occasions during the Obama presidency. It seems reasonable to conclude that if American military personnel are involved in military operations aimed at rescuing foreign nationals from pirates, Congress would have a legitimate role and voice in defining and regulating the military's behavior in this context. Moreover, President Obama has specifically noted that piracy has become an "extraordinary" threat to U.S. national security, which ostensibly means that Congress should play a regulatory role in evaluating such a threat and determining an appropriate response. The Obama administration's actions on the Indian Ocean have entailed repeated military operations, and they have not been confined to a single and immediate need for quick defensive or protective military action but rather have been part of a much larger set of policy decisions to combat pirates. Thus, a good case can be made that Congress's role to "define and punish piracies" applies in this new age of piracy, but Congress, as will become evident, has devoted little attention to the issue and, as in other cases of presidential military action, has largely allowed the commander in chief to address the threat as his administration chooses.

Congressional Involvement in Modern Antipiracy

During President Obama's first term, most members of Congress gave the issue of piracy little policy attention. To be sure, in 2009 a number of congressional committee hearings were held on the piracy challenge in the aftermath of the U.S. Navy SEAL operation to rescue Captain Richard Phillips.[28] No committee hearings that dealt exclusively with piracy were held in 2010 and 2012, and only two hearings on the issue were held in 2011. Thus, congressional oversight of antipiracy policy and action was quite limited in scope and, as will be evident, limited in substance as well.[29]

The first major congressional hearing held on piracy was led by the House Subcommittee on Coast Guard and Maritime Transportation of the Committee on Transportation and Infrastructure. Over the course of 2009, this subcommittee was the most active on the issue. Most of its attention prior to the *Maersk* incident in April 2009 focused on the threat of piracy as well as on possible solutions for dealing with piracy. Almost no attention was devoted to the navy's actual authority to carry out military operations in response to piracy, although the navy, when queried on the issue of authority to use force, made clear its belief that military action was a perfectly legitimate response to a pirate's attack. One revealing exchange came between ranking subcommittee minority member Frank LoBiondo (R–N.J.) and Admiral Ted N. Branch.

> MR. LOBIONDO: Let us say that the SOS goes out, and somebody is in close proximity, some military asset is in close proximity. What do they then have the authority to do to the pirates?

ADMIRAL BRANCH: They have the authority to thwart the pirates' attack.

MR. LoBIONDO: What does that mean?

ADMIRAL BRANCH: That means to stop it.

MR. LoBIONDO: By Force?

ADMIRAL BRANCH: Yes, sir, By Force.

MR. LoBIONDO: Okay. Thank you, Mr. Chairman.[30]

Clearly, Admiral Branch felt that the navy can use force, and Congressman LoBiondo was comfortable with Branch's asserted authority and by implication saw no need to question further or challenge Branch's claim. No other authority or constitutional qualms were posed during this subcommittee hearing. Admiral Branch's views went unchallenged.

Much more congressional attention to piracy came in the aftermath of the U.S. Navy SEALs operation to rescue Captain Richard Phillips, when on April 22, 2009, the House of Representatives commended the SEALs' actions, the broader U.S. Navy support for the operation, and the crew of the *Maersk Alabama*.[31] This day provided the most extensive discussion of piracy on the House floor during the first term of Obama's presidency, which totaled about twenty minutes, and a congratulatory resolution passed in a voice vote. All members who spoke at the time expressed their strong sentiments for the resolution and thus in their own way called for aggressive military action against the pirates. Jim Langevin (D–R.I.) and Sheila Jackson-Lee (D–Tex.) called for "swift and immediate action against these pirates."[32] Congressman Mike Coffman (R–Colo.) took an additional step by calling for the Obama administration to place small groups of U.S. marines on U.S. flagged commercial vessels.[33]

Within this discussion, the most explicit statements related to President Obama's authority to conduct military actions against pirates came from the chair of the House Armed Services Committee, Ike Skelton (D–Mo.), who maintained that members of the "international coalition" may use their "superior force to continue to pursue these pirates. . . . The authorities needed to conduct such operations have already been provided in United Nations Security Council Regulations 1846 and 1851."[34] Skelton's deference to the commander in chief is notable for at least two reasons. First, Skelton, who was first elected to Congress in 1977, had made the case in 2006 that if the Democrats were elected to the majority in the midterm elections, as chair of the House Armed Services Committee he would favor "oversight, oversight, oversight!"[35] Although it was clear that Skelton was aware of Obama's actions and was following his conduct and in this sense was providing oversight, it is equally evident that he saw little need for Congress formally to authorize these actions through its own constitutional process. Moreover, Skelton made the case that two UN Security Council resolutions provided Obama with the legitimate authority to conduct military action against pirates. As established in the previous chapter, this argument contrasts with the legislative history of the UN Participation Act of 1945, in which it was made clear that U.S. membership in the UN would not supersede congressional authority. Equally important is that a senior party leader among the House Democrats, the chair of the House Armed Services Committee, saw no need to review the president's authority to conduct this operation. One week prior to the House floor discussion, Skelton had sent a letter to President Obama encouraging his administration to aggressively pursue pirates on land and at sea. In doing so, Skelton referenced the Constitution, noting that "Article 1, Section 8 of the U.S. Constitution requires no less."[36] Perhaps this statement indicates that as a member of Congress Skelton was calling upon the president to act, but under what precise authority is not clear.

Like Skelton, Speaker of the House Nancy Pelosi (D–Calif.) also complimented the skills of the Navy SEALs as well as Captain Phillips and his crew through her own issued statement. She noted that "Congress is committed to working with the Obama Administration and the international community to effectively combat piracy and to bring to justice those responsible," but otherwise she played no public role in advocating for additional oversight of the president.[37] Like Skelton, she offered no substantive input on this national-security threat or challenge to the actions taken to combat it.

Other constitutional or statutory discussions of the Obama administration's authority to act militarily are nearly nonexistent. One exception, however, is evident in the views of the then-chair of the House Subcommittee on Coast Guard and Maritime Transportation, Elijah Cummings (D–Md.), who called for the placement of American military personnel on any U.S. flagged ship. He also made the case that it was the U.S. Navy's duty to protect American shipping and that the navy was failing to do so.[38] Although Chairman Cummings was clearly an advocate for protecting U.S. interests, his view, much like Chairman Skelton's, suggests unlimited military discretion for President Obama and the U.S. Navy to use force at will. In 2009, Senator Frank Lautenberg (D–N.J.), chair of the Senate Commerce, Science, and Transportation Subcommittee on Surface Transportation and Merchant Marine Infrastructure, Safety, and Security, made a nearly identical argument, calling for increased attention from the U.S. Navy. "A timid approach will not do," he stated. "We need to take bold action to keep our seas and ship crews safe."[39]

Other members of Congress outside of committee hearings turned to other potential solutions to address the piracy issue. One of the more novel policy solutions came from congressman and former presidential candidate Ron Paul (R–Tex.). Paul maintained that Congress should exercise its constitutional powers to issue "letters of marque and reprisal" to private citizens such that they can independently use force to destroy and kill the piracy threat. Paul argued that the U.S. Navy is presently unable to patrol against these kinds of threats and that the authorization of private individuals to use force would prove to be a far greater deterrent to the pirates.[40] Speaking in support of Paul's proposal, analyst Eli Lehrer noted, "If we have 100 American wanna-be Rambos patrolling the seas, it's probably a good way of getting the job done."[41]

Later in 2009, Congressman Frank LoBiondo introduced legislation to grant legal immunity to civilians who use armed force upon being attacked by pirates. Merchant mariners would be permitted to harm or kill pirates and be free from any legal prosecution.[42] In the Senate, Mark Kirk (R–Ill.) was also especially aggressive in calling for stronger military and naval efforts to combat piracy. Kirk called his ideas the "Decatur Initiative," named after Lieutenant Stephen Decatur, who helped recapture and then destroy the USS *Philadelphia* in 1804 after it was taken captive by pirates in Tripoli. Decatur's daring actions eliminated the possibility that the *Philadelphia* could be used against the United States. Kirk similarly wanted the U.S. Navy to be increasingly empowered to use force against Somali pirates and introduced his ideas on more than one occasion in 2011 as well.[43]

Others also expressed concern over piracy. Senator Russ Feingold (D–Wisc.) in 2009 called for greater international cooperation to address the piracy threat, although he expressed his skepticism of military solutions to the problem.[44] Congressman Ted Poe (R–Tex.) also expressed concern over the growing piracy threat, though he mostly just issued a warning to the pirates with implied threats of more intense military action, without advancing specific or new policy proposals.[45] In sum, nearly every member of the U.S. House of Representatives or the Senate who spoke out on the issue in the formal institutions of Congress called for more military action against pirates but raised no constitutional or statutory limitations on the president or the military for such actions. The House Democratic leadership, headed by Ike Skelton and Elijah Cummings, made the case for essentially unlimited presidential authority to eliminate the threat of piracy, devoid of any congressional authorization specifically provided in this context. Given that the senior party leaders in both the House and Senate rarely even commented on piracy, Skelton and Cummings, along with ranking minority subcommittee chair Frank LoBiondo, shaped nearly all of the discussion around this issue.

Political Implications

Over President Obama's first term, his administration authorized a number of daring and successful military operations against pirates. Equally important, the threat of Somali pirates waned considerably by 2012, which suggests the American and international military response paid high political and security dividends. Despite these policy successes, a good case can be made that Congress did not carry out its constitutional duties to "define and punish Piracies and Felonies Committed on the high Seas," as specified in the Constitution, in a manner that squares with meaningful oversight of the executive branch. Rather, Congress's actions, led by senior members of both bodies, provided the commander in chief with significant, if not all-empowering, discretion in determining how and when force is used abroad.

Congress's limited interest in piracy and oversight of the U.S. response to it have a number of negative constitutional and political implications. First, as established previously, "international law" on piracy, if it can be referred to in that manner, is far from clear.[46] Though State and Defense Department officials as well as some members of Congress frequently make sweeping references to piracy as a "universal crime under international law,"[47] widespread international disagreement exists over how to handle pirates and over what rights a pirate may have. Countries vary significantly on this aspect of international law. In reality, little is "universal" from an international legal perspective. Due to such legal ambiguity and especially given the Obama administration's ongoing willingness to use military force, it makes sense for Congress to exercise more meaningfully its explicit constitutional power in its interactions with the president on this matter.

There is existing international legal authorization for the use of force in the case of piracy; for example, the UN Security Council has approved the use of force to address piracy. The UN's intervention is interesting for at least two reasons. First, the Security Council's actions suggest that international law is not clear on piracy and the use of force. If piracy truly were a "universal crime" against all, which then ostensibly permits military force to be used against pirates at will, as some suggest, why then is Security Council action even necessary? In effect, the Security Council's action supports the argument that international law is not clear on piracy and that states are not automatically permitted to implement military solutions to face this problem. Second, the UN Participation Act of 1945 clearly established that Congress did not give away its power to check the president even when the commander in chief has UN approval to use force. U.S. membership in the UN did not eliminate Congress's constitutional role to check the president, and in this respect a UN Chapter VII authorization to use force invites congressional intervention, oversight, and ultimately domestic approval.[48] In sum, UN activities that relate to U.S. military action by definition invite congressional input, oversight, and, most important, authorization votes, which did not occur in U.S. military responses to piracy during Obama's first presidential term.

Apart from the legal and constitutional reasons for heightened congressional involvement in piracy, it is also clear that U.S. military actions against pirates can generate bilateral tensions with close allies if those allies take a different view of the proper response to piracy. Perhaps the best example of such tension came after the death of Wu Lai-yu, the captain of a Taiwan fishing vessel captured by Somali pirates in 2011. He was killed when the USS *Stephen W. Groves,* which had come to the vessel's assistance, engaged militarily with the pirates who had overtaken this vessel. Upon his death, Wu Lai-yu was buried at sea, though the Taiwanese government was not notified of the burial until ten days after the incident. All of these actions generated considerable tension between the United

States and Taiwan, normally very close allies.[49] Congress's absence from such debates again suggests legislative abdication on this issue, in which President Obama and the Department of Defense fully control U.S. foreign policy. The deference is especially interesting given that the U.S. military was in this case being used to assist a foreign national in need, as the U.S. Navy has done in a number of instances. Such behavior seems to contrast sharply even with the behavior of President Thomas Jefferson, who gave the U.S. Navy some discretion in dealing with pirates but did not send American military personnel abroad to assist and protect foreign states' merchant interests.

Though some members of Congress and perhaps the Obama administration may retort that current U.S. law permits the president to use U.S. ships in antipiracy operations, it is also not self-evident that the basic "law" shaping this argument, much of which was written in 1823, is appropriate for the scope of modern antipiracy operations, given the expanding national-security threat and the array of military operations that have been used to address piracy, including U.S. military assistance to foreign nationals. In this context, the general constitutional notion of checks and balances—especially with respect to the commander in chief—ostensibly justifies greater congressional oversight on this issue.

Moreover, the question remains open under existing U.S. law regarding how much force the commander in chief can use against pirates and whether the president can legally and constitutionally wage war against them, as some commentators have suggested.[50] It seems unlikely that existing U.S. domestic antipiracy law is the equivalent of a Gulf of Tonkin Resolution against pirates, which would permit the president to use as much force as he pleased. Greater legislative oversight not only has the political advantage of helping to clarify existing law but also squares more closely with the constitutional principle of checks and balances.

4

Obama's Military Strikes on Libya

The U.S. and NATO use of force in Libya in 2011 was the first new war for President Obama. Although Obama significantly enlarged the U.S. military presence in Afghanistan and dramatically increased the use of predator drone strikes against Taliban and al-Qaeda operatives, these military operations still fell under the broad umbrella of the George W. Bush administration's foreign policy and the previous authorization of the use of force against terrorists in 2001. The strikes in Libya were different, however, and produced a more assertive response from some members of Congress. In his effort to justify presidential insulation from congressional oversight during the strikes, Obama advanced a legal argument with respect to the WPR that proved to be controversial to many members of Congress, constitutional law experts, and even top legal advisors in his own administration.[1] In perhaps his most poignant statements about war powers, akin to President George W. Bush's reference to himself as "the decider" for U.S. military policy, Obama later dismissively referenced congressional concerns over his asserted war powers authority in Libya as "noise about the process."[2]

Apart from Libya's being an excellent test case of the Obama administration's views on war powers and Congress's response to a novel military action in his presidency, this use of force is also especially intriguing given that a number of substantive political and legal congressional challenges were advanced against the commander in chief. However, in the end Congress, as it has done so many times before, chose to follow Obama's lead and avoided questions surrounding the constitutionality of the president's conduct.

Some members of Congress did mount considerable challenges, yet this opposition had little impact on how American forces were used or on Obama's foreign policy. These legislative war powers challenges were generally discouraged, co-opted, or simply opposed by the House and Senate leadership of both parties, which worked to keep Congress's constitutional and political responsibility for the strikes limited and tertiary. Speaker of the House John Boehner (R–Ohio) played a critical role in this process of curtailing significant constitutional challenges to the commander in chief and instead continued the practice of congressional deference to the president in the decision making on military conflicts. Among the cases addressed in this book, the Libya case provides an especially illustrative example of how Congress's leaders foster abdication to the commander in chief and at times work to prevent Congress's assumption of responsibility for the use of force abroad.

Air Strikes on Libya and Presidential "Authority"

U.S. military engagement in Libya began on March 19, 2011, when the U.S. Navy launched a number of Tomahawk missiles at Libyan air defenses. In his public address later that day, President Obama noted that the U.S. actions were taken to enforce UN Security Council Resolution 1973. He added that "I've acted after consulting with my national security team, and Republican and Democratic leaders of Congress."[3] Much as previous presidents have done, he later officially informed members of Congress of his military actions through written notification, repeating that his actions were authorized by the UN Security Council and that he was acting under his constitutional authority as commander in chief and in accordance with his constitutional power to conduct foreign relations.[4]

At a press briefing three days later, Deputy National Security Advisor for Strategic Communications Ben Rhodes elaborated on the degree of congressional involvement in the decision to strike Muammar Qaddafi's forces. Rhodes noted that on the day prior to the strikes, either members of the bicameral congressional leadership came to the White House to speak with President Obama, or the president spoke with them over the phone. After these conversations, officials from the Departments of

Defense and State and the intelligence agencies spoke to some individuals on the "appropriate [congressional] oversight committees." Rhodes added that the president's actions very closely comported with a Senate resolution passed on March 1 that was substantively similar to UN Security Council Resolution 1973, which authorized military enforcement of a no-fly zone over Libya. In addition, Rhodes noted accurately that Obama's constitutional arguments differed little from President Bill Clinton's constitutional claims in 1995, when the United States and NATO allies used force in Bosnia absent explicit authorization from Congress.[5] In this respect, President Obama fell in line with his predecessors, relying on UN Security Council decisions and traditional claims utilized by presidents when seeking to use force abroad without Congress's approval.

Congressional Assertions of War Powers and "Noise about the Process"

Prior to the start of the air strikes, a number of congressional committee hearings were held regarding the crisis in Libya, which clearly demonstrates some congressional engagement on the issue. In addition, on March 1, 2011, the U.S. Senate passed Senate Resolution 85, which called upon Qaddafi to end his human rights violations and pushed the UN Security Council to support a "possible imposition of a no-fly zone over Libyan territory." In introducing this proposal, Senator Charles Schumer (D–N.Y.) added a no-fly provision over Libya to the broader Senate Resolution 85.[6] Although Schumer's proposal had the sponsorship of eleven senators, no committee hearings dealt with this resolution, and no Senate floor debate occurred. Members of the Senate were informed of the Libya–UN Security Council addendum approximately eleven minutes before Schumer's language was implemented and passed, in part because of Schumer's request for the unanimous-consent procedure. This measure was discussed on the Senate floor for approximately thirty-five seconds.[7] Thus, although the Senate certainly did take some action on Libya, it is difficult to argue that these steps represent a serious legislative effort to endorse military action against Qaddafi. Nonetheless, as noted earlier, Deputy National Security Advisor for Strategic Communications Ben Rhodes maintained that the Senate's actions provided some legislative backing for Obama's military actions. The Justice Department's Office of

Legal Counsel similarly maintained that Senate Resolution 85 provided some degree of legal justification for Obama's actions; that the U.S. use of force did not amount to a "war" in the constitutional sense and therefore did not require congressional approval; and that Obama's actions had historical precedent, which in the office's view permitted the president to act without specific congressional authorization.[8]

Some immediate responses came from members of Congress, especially Senators John McCain (R–Ariz.) and Lindsey Graham (R–S.C.), who were quite supportive of the use of force, though they included the critique that they wished Obama had acted sooner.[9] These voices, however, were soon overwhelmed by those of other members of Congress who expressed serious concerns over the constitutionality of the strikes and certainly over the decision-making process that led to the strikes. In many members' views, this process included only tertiary consideration of Congress's opinions on both the policy and constitutional process prior to the strikes. In the Senate, Richard Lugar (R–Ind.) and Rand Paul (R–Ky.) maintained that the president was using the U.S. military without explicit constitutional authority.[10] Lugar noted that "we need to have a debate in the Congress on a declaration of war against the Libya state. . . . A no-fly zone is a military action. That requires the advice and consent of Congress."[11] Paul advanced his concerns early and often on the Senate floor and reached out to national media on a number of occasions to argue that Obama had acted unconstitutionally. He made the argument that Congress had made itself "irrelevant" by not asserting its war powers authority.[12]

Some of the most pointed criticism from the House of Representatives came from freshman congressman Justin Amash (R–Mich.), who circulated a letter among members of the House calling the strikes unconstitutional and demanding an end to U.S. military participation in the conflict. This letter was followed with the introduction of the bill for his "Reclaim Act" on March 29, 2011, which was intended to reassert Congress's war powers on Libya.[13] Amash's action, coupled with the many proposals that followed soon after, demonstrated a level of congressional war powers assertiveness near the onset of a presidential military operation that was uncommon in the recent history of U.S. use of force. Whether in response to President Ronald Reagan's 1983 military operation in Grenada, President George H. W. Bush's invasion of Panama in 1989, or the U.S. military actions in Iraq when the Clinton administration used extensive force across a number of years, Congress was considerably less active—and nearly silent on war powers in some cases—than in the constitutional questions it raised in 2011 over Obama's strikes.[14]

As the weeks passed and the strikes continued, the interest in Congress's war powers increased, especially as the sixty- and then ninety-day time limit imposed by the WPR approached and passed.[15] In May 2011, Congressman John Conyers (D–Mich.) introduced a resolution that prohibited President Obama from using American ground troops in the Libyan military operation; it passed overwhelmingly in a vote of 416 to 5.[16] Congressman Dennis Kucinich (D–Ohio), who has a long, consistent, and nonpartisan history as an advocate of congressional war powers, advanced the most aggressive effort.[17] Kucinich raised questions from the start of the operation, though momentum grew over time for his position that Obama had acted without constitutional authority. His resolution, voted on June 3, 2011, called for the removal of all American military forces from the Libya operation in fifteen days. This resolution failed by a vote of 148 to 265, though it had considerable bipartisan support, with 61 House Democrats voting in favor of it.[18] A resolution on the same day offered by Speaker of the House John Boehner, however, gained the House's support. Boehner's resolution called for the president to report back to the Congress in fourteen days over many aspects of the operation, including the purpose and cost of the strikes.[19] At this same time, in another war powers challenge, Kucinich and a bipartisan group of nine other House members turned to the courts to request a ruling on the constitutionality of Obama's actions.[20]

The final major surge of congressional activism on war powers authority in the Libya case came in late June and early July 2011 in the aftermath of the Obama administration's position that its military actions in Libya did not fall under the jurisdiction of the WPR.[21] Harold Koh, the State Department's top legal advisor, and Robert Bauer, the White House counsel, maintained that the United States was not involved in "hostilities" and therefore was not subject to the legislative limitations outlined by the WPR, which indicates that anytime the United States is engaged in "hostilities," legislative approval is required to continue the military operation. Their report argued that because the operation in Libya did not entail the presence of American ground forces and there was no active exchange of fire between Libya and U.S. forces, the standard set forth in the WPR had not been met.[22] Like his predecessors, though in different circumstances, Obama similarly utilized this semantic tactic regarding the definition of the term *hostilities* to insulate the administration from Congress and the WPR, though there was no factual doubt that the United States was conducting sustained and ongoing missile strikes on Libya. It is worth noting that there was considerable debate within the administration over this position, the top lawyers in the Defense Department and in the Justice Department's Office of Legal Counsel maintaining that the United States was indeed engaged in hostilities.[23]

A number of legislative efforts followed in the House of Representatives aimed at limiting U.S. participation in the military operation. Freshman representative Joe Heck (R–Nev.) introduced a resolution that called for the removal of all funding for any U.S. activity involving military strikes but retained funding for various support activities.[24] His resolution failed. A contrasting resolution offered by Congressman Alcee L. Hastings (D–Fla.) that called for the House to authorize air strikes against Libya was also defeated. Thus, the House was unwilling to restrict funding for the operation, but at the same time it was also unwilling to express its support for the operation.[25]

A similar pattern was repeated on July 7, 2011, when the House took five votes related to Libya. Justin Amash, Scott Rigell (R–Va.), and Louie Gohmert (R–Tex.) introduced similar measures that called for the elimination of funding for U.S. and/or NATO military action in Libya; all of these measures failed. The House successfully passed a resolution that barred any funding from going to support any nongovernmental forces in Libya. In addition, it also voted to bar any funding that would allow the president to "contravene the War Powers Resolution" by expanding the operation.[26] Thus, at best, the House sent very mixed messages regarding its position on Obama's military actions in Libya. The House was again unwilling to vote in favor of the operation, but in three very similar ways it indicated that it was *not* willing to cut funding for U.S. military participation in the operation. In effect, the House both supported and opposed the use of force. Nonetheless, Obama's military actions in Libya generated an uncommon and heightened level of congressional activism on constitutional war powers. Many members of the House especially made multiple and sustained efforts to limit the Obama administration, and these efforts also had bipartisan backing. Yet although many resolutions were advanced, none can be viewed as a substantial limitation on the president's ability to conduct the war. Much of this institutional deference can be explained by examining the roles played by the House and Senate leadership.

Explaining Congress's Institutional Deference

As Stephen Weissman has argued, Congress's inability or unwillingness to assert its institutional and constitutional foreign-policy powers can often be traced to the absence of congressional leadership on the issue.[27] In the Libya case, congressional leadership was present, although it was exercised to *prevent* constitutional questions and other more assertive policy actions aimed at limiting President Obama's military operation in Libya. Despite the limited notification provided to members of Congress prior to the strikes, some 7,725 U.S. air sorties with 397 different strikes as well as 145 predator drone attacks over the course of seven months, and the presidential claim that the United States was not engaged in hostilities, Congress's unwillingness either to endorse or to oppose this operation explicitly can largely be explained by the actions of Congress's institutional leaders.[28] Speaker of the House John Boehner and a number of key senior foreign-policy elites in the U.S. Senate, including Senators John Kerry (D–Mass.), John McCain, Carl Levin (D–Mich.), and Harry Reid (D–Nev.), were central in this process that granted the president discretion to initiate and conduct this war as he wished.

In the House of Representatives, from the operation's onset Boehner made few efforts to insert the House into a debate over the constitutionality of Obama's military conduct. Although he expressed concern by calling for more operational and strategic details about the mission, he did not explicitly object to the constitutionality of Obama's action. More than a month into the strikes, the House leadership was still unwilling to permit an open debate on the House floor to discuss the merits or constitutionality of the operation, which continued into late May 2011.[29] Congressman Tim Johnson (R–Ill.) maintains that Boehner as well as Rules Committee chair David Drier (R–Calif.) used a variety of legislative maneuvers to actively suppress all war powers challenges. Though the Democratic leadership lacked legislative power, Johnson also maintains that minority leader Nancy Pelosi (D–Calif.) and minority whip Steny Hoyer (D–Md.) were complicit with the Republican leadership in curbing Kucinich's efforts.[30]

With the sixty-day WPR timeline having passed, limited concern expressed by House leaders in that period, and pressure building in favor of Kucinich's efforts to cut funding for the operation, Boehner injected himself into the House debate. In contrast to Kucinich's resolution, Boehner offered his own resolution on Libya, which was critical of the president but still avoided any constitutional responsibility for the operation. His resolution chastised the president for not having more dialogue with Congress and required that Obama send Congress additional information regarding the cost and objectives of the operation within fourteen days. In doing so, Boehner was able to dampen the enthusiasm for Kucinich's resolution and in this sense to successfully co-opt Kucinich's more assertive resolution.[31]

Libya was not the first operation in which Boehner was unwilling to assert a constitutional position on Congress's war powers. Though some individuals in the press and Congress highlighted the different views Obama as commander in chief held on war powers compared to the stated positions he had previously taken as a senator, White House press secretary Jay Carney noted that Boehner himself had stated in 1999 that he viewed the WPR as "constitutionally suspect."[32] In addition, prior to his speakership, Boehner was closely involved in the 1995 Republican House leadership debate over President Clinton's military actions in Yugoslavia, which culminated in the deployment of 20,000 American troops in a NATO peacekeeping operation in Bosnia. The House eventually voted to "support the troops, but not the policy," which was at that time a novel way to express patriotism for U.S. forces while avoiding any constitutional position in the actual deployment of thousands of Americans abroad.[33] Boehner, who at that time served as chairman of the Republican conference, and Speaker of the House Newt Gingrich (R–Ga.)—despite their opposition to Clinton's policy—were unwilling to cut funding for the operation and helped the "support the troops but not the policy" resolution win.[34] On Libya, Boehner recycled a similar approach, which avoided the question of whether Obama had authority to conduct the operation and prevented the assertive measures to remove funding, while simultaneously allowing the president to continue the operation without explicit legislative approval.

Boehner was not the only House leader to resist constitutional assertions of Congress's war powers. Minority leader Nancy Pelosi made no efforts to garner support for either Boehner's resolution or the more aggressive resolutions offered by Amash and Kucinich. She stood solidly behind President Obama and did not challenge the constitutionality of his actions or his interpretation of the WPR.[35] House Foreign Affairs Committee chair Ilena Ros-Lehtinen (R–Fla.) expressed constitutional qualms regarding Obama's actions but at the same time played a leading role in helping to defeat Kucinich's actions, arguing that his resolution would harm NATO and the mission in Afghanistan. In contrast to Congressmen Amash and Kucinich, she maintained that "Congress needs to strongly exert its prerogatives under War Powers . . . but do so in a prudent and responsible manner that protects legitimate national security interests."[36] Thus, like Boehner, she was content to criticize but unwilling to issue a constitutional challenge to the commander in chief. Nor did she use her position as chair of the House Foreign Affairs Committee to challenge the constitutionality of Obama's conduct.

One significant political factor in the debates witnessed in both the House and the Senate was the degree of freshman activity on this issue. Some research indicates that the longer a member's tenure is in Congress, the greater his or her prospects are for successfully passing legislation. Experienced legislators are found to be more skillful in knowing how to garner the necessary support to see their resolutions become law.[37] In the case of Libya, some of the more assertive efforts witnessed in the spring and summer of 2011 were led by freshman members, including Congressmen Justin Amash, Joe Heck, and Scott Rigell, so it not surprising that these efforts failed. Freshman senator Rand Paul, who was the loudest and most consistent voice for Congress's war powers in the Senate, was similarly ineffective.

Apart from the heightened freshman presence on war powers, some of this assertiveness was also captured by new House members associated with the national Tea Party movement who had gained electoral success in the 2010 midterm elections.[38] These members have stricter interpretations of the Constitution and thus appear to interpret more conservatively the Constitution's War Clause, which gives to Congress the power to declare war. Congressman Ron Paul, whose views closely coincide with Tea Party enthusiasts, has been one of the most consistent advocates for

Congress's war powers during his full tenure in the House.[39] In the Senate, a number of Tea Party enthusiasts—including Rand Paul; Mike Lee (R–Utah) and Jim DeMint (R–S.C.), the founders of the Senate Tea Party Caucus; and Senator Ron Johnson (R–Wisc.)—were supporters of Paul's calls for congressional war powers.[40] It may also be that these freshman Republicans came to Congress with heightened levels of partisanship and thus were even more inclined to challenge the president than were more veteran House and Senate Republicans. Regardless of their motivations, these freshman, Republican, Tea Party–affiliated members were only in their third month in office when the strikes ensued and had virtually no legislative experience and thus an absence of legislative skills necessary to challenge their senior party leaders.

In the Senate, from the start of the operation John McCain was a prominent voice in favor of military action and at times called for even more aggressive action. As the momentum in the House grew for Kucinich's and Amash's war powers proposals, McCain directed his criticism at the House for standing in President Obama's way. He argued that such checking efforts were helping to rescue Qaddafi from a forthcoming defeat.[41] Later in July 2011, McCain referred to Congress's efforts to limit the commander in chief as "deeply disturbing."[42]

As demonstrated in chapter 6, McCain has a long legacy of protecting the commander in chief regardless of the military conflict in question. Yet it is also important to recognize his senior status in the Senate as well as his leadership role as ranking minority member of the Armed Services Committee. In this respect, especially given his distinguished military career prior to his life in elected office, a case can be made that he has some ability to shape the national debate on military issues, which he sought to do in the Libya conflict by immediately arguing in national media outlets that Obama's actions were correct, though just perhaps too late.

John Kerry, chairman of the Senate Foreign Relations Committee in 2011, played a similar role in limiting congressional interference on Libya. Kerry, whose war powers record is also discussed in greater detail in chapter 6, came to national prominence during the Vietnam War when he called upon Congress to exercise its constitutional powers vis-à-vis President Richard Nixon. Like McCain, Kerry has also played a leading role in protecting commanders in chief from congressional pressure.

Regarding Libya, Kerry very early on stated his support for military action and advocated for Congress to be patient with Obama as the strikes proceeded.[43] As the operation advanced, Kerry came to President Obama's defense to back the administration's claim that the United States was not engaged in hostilities and therefore that the WPR did not apply. When pressed more specifically on the WPR, he noted, "I do not think our limited involvement rises to the level of hostilities defined by the War Powers Resolution."[44] He later added in a news interview: "I really do know something about the War Powers Act. . . . It was not created with drones in mind or with the kind of technology and anti-terror conflicts that we're facing today."[45]

On June 28, 2011, at a Senate Foreign Relations Committee hearing that focused specifically on the question of war powers and Libya, Kerry again defended the Obama administration and went to some lengths to support the administration's interpretation of the WPR. He directed very pointed criticism toward Senator Bob Corker (R–Tenn.), who had raised concerns over the administration's legal defense of the strikes.[46] Moreover, soon after Kucinich's failed efforts in the House in June 2011 to limit funding for the operation, Senators Kerry and McCain joined forces to introduce a Senate resolution that authorized the president "to continue the limited use of the United States armed forces in Libya, in support of United States national security policy interests" for one year. Levin, another senior senator and chairman of the Senate Armed Services Committee, was a co-sponsor of the resolution.[47] Like Kerry, Levin had been a patient advocate for the president, noting that the Obama administration needed more time for the military operation to work, nor did he advocate any meaningful assertion of Congress's war powers during the conflict.[48]

Senate majority leader Harry Reid, much like McCain, also defended President Obama's asserted constitutional authority as commander in chief. Reid criticized members of the House of Representatives for raising the WPR, viewing these efforts as partisan attacks on the president, even though Kucinich, Amash, and others had considerable bipartisan backing for their efforts. Reid also argued that Obama's actions did not violate the WPR.[49] Senate majority whip Richard Durbin (D–Ill.) expressed some concern with Obama's interpretation of the term *hostilities* as used in the WPR but also introduced a resolution that supported Obama's actions through December 30, 2011. Durbin's resolution called for a restriction on ground troops, although Obama had stated from the start that ground troops would not be used.[50] Durbin, like other senior senators and party leaders, including Kerry, McCain, Reid, and Levin, chose not to advance a war powers challenge to the president and did not associate himself with the more aggressive efforts led by Senator Paul. The Senate Democratic leadership also chose not to bring the Kerry–McCain–Levin resolution forward for a vote during the height of the House opposition, nor did Durbin's resolution advance, which suggests a leadership concern that unwanted and more substantive debate would occur with these resolutions and that it was thus better to table them.

The most senior senator to express concern over Obama's constitutional conduct was Richard Lugar, the ranking minority member of the Senate Foreign Relations Committee, who had a distinguished record in the 1980s and 1990s for shaping major foreign-policy and strategic directions for the United States.[51] From the start of the Libya operation, Lugar argued that Obama needed explicit legislative authorization to conduct the military strikes.[52] However, he found no allies among the Senate leadership.

Presidential Leadership, Congressional Deference, and Its Implications

The findings in this chapter indicate that in the Libya case President Barack Obama, much like previous U.S. presidents—including George H. W. Bush, Bill Clinton, and George W. Bush—continued to assert wide constitutional powers as commander in chief and in effect made the determinative decisions for when and if the United States would use force abroad. Congress's leaders, however, were also central in shaping the political process that led to its deference to the commander in chief during the military strikes in Libya. Congressional leaders were critical in limiting floor debate on war powers in both the House and the Senate. Committee chairs also helped lead the way in supporting presidential claims or chose not to challenge the commander in chief's asserted authority. Most significantly, Speaker of the House John Boehner played an instrumental role in co-opting Congressman Dennis Kucinich's effort to remove funding for the military operation. Congress's leaders managed to criticize the president but at the same time to avoid any constitutional responsibility for this use of force. Though institutional deference to the president remains the norm, the significant role of Congress's bipartisan leaders in preventing substantive checks against the commander in chief provides a more complete understanding of *why* deference occurred in this case.

At the same time, the congressional–executive interplay over Libya was much different from the interplay regarding previous U.S. military actions abroad. In this case, the House especially witnessed a surge of bipartisan activism on war powers that had no recent historical comparison. Many members of Congress, both Democrat and Republican, were active on war powers and viewed the Constitution's War Clause as a real power that the Congress must exercise. This assertiveness, however, came primarily from freshman members with little to no legislative expertise and from members of Congress at the more extreme ends of their political parties—namely, Congressmen Dennis Kucinich and Justin Amash and Senator Rand Paul.[53] Legislative activism on war powers was present and bipartisan, but it was not enough to defeat congressional party leaders' preferences.

What remained the same with respect to this use of force was the Obama administration's view that the president is the sole decision maker for the use of military force abroad. Despite extensive use of air power and drone strikes against targets that could not be viewed as fitting under the previous 2001 authorization to use force against terrorists, President Obama maintained that this use of force did not constitute a war or "hostilities" and thus was not within Congress's jurisdiction to limit.[54] Similar to its actions in Afghanistan and implied in its dealings with pirates, the Obama administration viewed itself as the primary decision maker for U.S. military action in Libya. In its view, such decisions are not intended for Congress.

The use of force in Libya is also interesting given that the House approved a resolution offered by Congressman John Conyers that prohibited the use of American ground forces in Libya. In addition, the House also voted to prohibit any U.S. aid from going to anti-Qaddafi forces. A number of media reports, however, indicate the presence of CIA operatives on the ground in Libya, who helped identify targets for NATO strikes and sought to learn more about anti-Qaddafi forces.[55] Although such intelligence activity is not exactly the same as having American military personnel on the ground, it certainly resulted in assistance to the rebels and consisted of Americans on the ground who advanced the U.S. military mission. It appears that these operatives were on the ground prior to the initiation of U.S. military force, but there is also no indication that the CIA presence was removed after the congressional resolutions. It seems more likely than not that CIA operatives remained on the ground, which would lend further credence to the argument that it is the president, not Congress, who makes U.S. military policy.

The presence of congressional partisanship is another variable to consider in this case. The active war powers opposition present in the Senate came primarily from a small group of Republicans. Moreover, few Republicans were willing to support the president. In contrast, the Democratic leadership in the House and Senate stood solidly behind the president and generally backed President Obama's asserted war powers authority or chose not to challenge him publicly. Some of the most aggressive challenges to President Obama also came from freshman Republicans. By these measures, partisanship is certainly a relevant variable for understanding both congressional opposition and deference to the president. Yet given Republican leaders' unwillingness to place limitations on President Obama and sixty-one House Democrats' challenge to President Obama's war powers claims, the role of both the House's and Senate's leadership appears instrumental in limiting Congress's war powers authorization role. The more critical point evident here is that congressional leaders of *both* parties worked to avoid constitutional and political authority for this use of force. Thus, partisanship, as measured by support or opposition to one's political party in power at the White House, provides only a partial and limited understanding of the war powers interplay in this case. Most members of Congress and all of its primary leaders in both parties sought to avoid constitutional responsibility for the military action.

It may also be argued that perhaps most members of Congress actually believe that the president was authorized to use force absent congressional approval in Libya. Certainly, Senators McCain and Kerry held this view. Such an argument, however, seems difficult to accept if the idea of checks and balances has any real constitutional merit. As Senator Dick Durbin noted—though did not act upon—the Obama administration's argument that the United States was not engaged in hostilities failed to pass the "straight face test."[56] As part of the NATO coalition, the United States conducted nearly 400 different air strikes, 145 predator drone attacks, and almost 8,000 air missions. Rather than accept the view that most in Congress felt that President Obama was authorized to conduct military operations in Libya, it seems more convincing to conclude that Congress and its leaders excel in finding ways to avoid taking political and constitutional responsibility for the use of force abroad.

In sum, despite Obama's claims for a newly interpreted WPR to justify air power and drone strikes, and despite the sustained application of U.S. force in Libya for nearly seven months, congressional leaders managed to avoid a specific vote either to authorize or to prevent military action. Bipartisan congressional assertiveness in the House of Representatives and the efforts to apply the WPR, coupled with the more limited opposition in the Senate, were unable to move congressional leaders to challenge President Obama's constitutional claims as commander in chief, all of which squares with the general practice in U.S. foreign-policy making and with a Congress that grants the commander in chief wide policy discretion in determining if and when U.S. military force will be used abroad.

5

The Hunt for Joseph Kony

On October 14, 2011, President Barack Obama informed congressional leaders that approximately one hundred American military personnel would be deployed to four African states—the Central African Republic, the Democratic Republic of the Congo, South Sudan, and Uganda—in an effort to eliminate the Lord's Resistance Army (LRA), led by Joseph Kony. The LRA was formed in 1987 when after a government coup in Uganda led by Yoweri Museveni another government opposition movement led by Kony's alleged relative, Alice Lakwena, was defeated by Musevini's forces. Kony's forces are known for their brutality in slaughtering villagers and kidnapping children. The LRA also presses the kidnapped children to commit atrocities against their own families if they wish to remain alive or to avoid mutilation. In addition, sexual slavery among the children is a common practice in Kony's group. In carrying out such atrocities, Kony maintains that he is guided by the Holy Spirit, carrying out his own vision of Christianity.[1]

On October 14, 2011, when President Obama announced his decision to provide U.S. military support to these four countries in combating the LRA, some of these troops had already been deployed and had been sent with "appropriate combat equipment." Obama noted that these forces "will not themselves engage LRA forces unless necessary for self defense." He added that he was informing Congress of these actions "as part of my efforts to keep the Congress fully informed, consistent with the War Powers Resolution," and that he was carrying out Congress's legislative desires by fulfilling the expectations of the Lord's Resistance Army Disarmament and Northern Uganda Recovery Act of 2009.[2]

The legislative process that led to the act's passage was unique and in many respects contrasts sharply with Congress's traditional role in U.S. military and security policy formation. It also does not square perfectly with the norms of behavior witnessed in President Obama's first term with respect to Afghanistan, pirates, and Libya. By playing a much more assertive role than it traditionally has, Congress pushed President Obama to develop a comprehensive strategy to eliminate the LRA, which included the potential for the president to provide military support to African militaries. Though Senator Russ Feingold (D–Wisc.) later maintained that "our legislation did not authorize the use of force by American troops anywhere," the actual legislation provided the president with considerable discretion to determine how to best confront the LRA.[3]

This chapter examines the legislative and political process that led to the passage of the LRA Disarmament and Northern Uganda Recovery Act. It is an important case to consider given that, like actions taken to deal with the Somali pirates and the strikes on Qaddafi, it was a unique decision by the Obama administration to actively deploy military forces. Moreover, this decision was not simply an extension of the Bush administration's policies; no such previous congressional authorization existed from the Bush administration era. Moreover, apart from demonstrating a degree of foreign-policy assertiveness often not witnessed from Congress, this issue is especially interesting given that it occurred in central Africa, where U.S. strategic interests are arguably perceived as less clear. Since the failed U.S. military operation in Somalia in 1993, Congress has rarely shown sustained or even marginal interest in a meaningful U.S. military ground deployment to Africa. Thus, the policy formation addressed here is unique and especially interesting for understanding why Congress became so active on a human rights concern that impacts so few Americans and has limited strategic interests to the United States.

At the same time, even though Congress did pass an act that granted Obama increased foreign-policy and military authority, a degree of deference was built into the legislative process that allowed members to avoid political responsibility for Obama's eventual actions. Despite Congress's "activity," in many respects it also deferred to the commander in chief in determining how to resolve and address this problem. This chapter provides some support for the previous scholarship on congressional assertiveness in foreign policy, but it also addresses a number of case-specific political variables that were significant in the passage of this legislation. Among these factors, the multiple roles played by nongovernmental organizations (NGOs), Kony's identity as a "terrorist," and the legislative process used to pass this act are central to understanding not only why Joseph Kony and the LRA generated so much congressional attention but also how congressional deference was again present in this case.

Congressional Foreign-Policy Activism

Thus far, the previous chapters have argued that Congress often defers to the commander in chief and that this deference is often orchestrated by senior members of Congress regardless of political party. The case discussed in this chapter has important differences but also some critical similarities. To understand how it fits with the previous cases of congressional abdication, it is important to understand the wider scope of research on U.S. foreign-policy making beyond war powers, where analysts have established a more active presence for members of Congress. By using a broader set of previous scholarship on Congress and foreign policy, one may better understand why Congress so actively targeted the LRA and pushed the president for a new strategy. Within this scholarship, three bodies of research, some of which overlap, address when and why Congress may engage in the broader foreign-policy-making process.

Among the principal motivations for policy activism is the desire to get reelected. David Mayhew most famously maintained that members of Congress focus nearly all of their activities at securing future electoral victories.[4] A number of recent studies suggest that members direct their foreign-policy interests to issues that will be attractive to their constituencies or to those issue areas that have electoral benefits and rewards.[5]

A second body of scholarship on U.S. foreign policy maintains that partisanship helps explain a congressional member's behavior and that this partisanship may overlap with his or her electoral interests. Though considerable debate exists within this area of research, many studies have found that a member's party affiliation is an important predictor for his or her stands on congressional foreign policy. Much of this research also points to an increasingly partisan Congress since the Vietnam War.[6]

Other research highlights the significant role that a Congress member's personal policy interests may have in driving his or her foreign-policy activism.[7] Members of Congress may have especially strong interests in specific trade issues, unique U.S. bilateral relationships, or perhaps a similar set of issues, such as U.S. foreign policy and human rights. It can be difficult analytically, however, to separate a member's personal policy interests from his or her electoral and district-level pressures. For example, research on membership in Congress's Human Rights Caucus finds evidence of both personal policy interests as well as a member's district preferences to explain his or her participation in this caucus.[8]

Though important differences remain in the findings in research on congressional foreign-policy involvement, especially regarding the degree of influence the factors identified here exercise on a member of Congress, much research suggests that electoral incentives, partisan politics, and personal policy interests offer useful insights for understanding why members of Congress engage in foreign policy. Thus, it is fair to hypothesize that in explaining Congress's foreign-policy activism with respect to the LRA, a reasonable analysis would find the presence of each of these factors. At the same time, given that Congress's actions on Joseph Kony entailed a military element, it seems reasonable to anticipate that some measure of deference to the executive would also be apparent in this case.

Electoral Pressures

At first glance, it seems counterintuitive to argue that electoral pressures drove members of Congress to address the human rights violations carried out by the LRA and Joseph Kony. To be sure, few question the notion that the LRA and Joseph Kony represent evil. Though the group is seen as having no more than two hundred "core combatants," it is estimated to have caused the internal displacement of 465,000 people and killed approximately 2,400 people in Central Africa in 2011, committing wide-scale human rights abuses in the process.[9]

However, from a strictly nationalistic perspective, the LRA represents a limited strategic threat to the United States. The LRA has not killed Americans and barely threatens close U.S. allies in the region. Though the International Criminal Court called for the arrests of Joseph Kony and other LRA leaders in 2005, and the United States included the LRA on its Terror Exclusion List in 2001, Kony's and the LRA's reach is localized to only portions of Central Africa. Moreover, the last major deployment of

American troops to Africa, which occurred in Somalia in 1992, resulted in military disaster for the United States, the loss of American lives, and deep political costs to the Clinton administration.[10] American military analysts maintain that though the United States has the highest military expenditures in the world and one of the most professionalized military forces, its military is stretched quite thin with too many deployments, and there is little preference for more military action abroad.[11] Thus, despite the clear and compelling humanitarian reasons for taking action against Kony and the LRA, strong strategic arguments existed for remaining disengaged from this central African problem.

In spite of these strategic and political arguments for letting African governments resolve this issue on their own, members of Congress still faced considerable public pressure to take action against Kony, which indicates some electoral incentives to respond to a mobilized electorate. In this case, assessing the importance of the NGO Invisible Children is critical for understanding grassroots pressure on members of Congress.

Invisible Children

Formed in 2003, Invisible Children was initially led by three university film students from California who sought to bring attention to the plight of Ugandan children who were the LRA's victims. In making its case to the public, this group used a short film, *Invisible Children: Rough Cut,* to educate Americans on political conditions in northern Uganda.[12] By 2008, Invisible Children had shown this film and other short documentaries to some "550 churches, 1,250 colleges and 1,100 high schools" and in the process had reached out to various audiences and encouraged political activism. Through these efforts, it connected with thousands of young Americans, who subsequently joined in the cause.[13] The group's founders were especially adept at generating support from young Christian evangelicals. Jason Russell, one of the founders, sought out Christian evangelical colleges, including Liberty University, to solicit their students' support. Invisible Children also successfully appealed to a number of conservative-leaning Christian organizations to help finance its movement.[14]

When the Invisible Children online video on Kony and the LRA went viral in March 2012 and reached approximately 97 million viewers, some indicators of the group's grassroots demographic base was illustrated.[15] In tracking the initial Twitter traffic employed to generate attention for this video, strong bases of support were identified in Oklahoma City; Noblesville, Indiana; Birmingham, Alabama; and Pittsburgh, with an especially strong foundation in Alabama. An examination of the user profiles among this Twitter activity provided evidence of a strong Christian element in that many Christian words or phrases were posted on the users' biographical profiles.[16] Though Invisible Children does not explicitly espouse religious themes, it was not uncommon to witness break-away prayer sessions at its rallies.[17] In short, this evidence suggests that Invisible Children successfully cultivated a strong and committed grassroots foundation among young Christian evangelicals in politically conservative-leaning areas of the United States.

Further evidence of the strength of Invisible Children's political support had appeared a few years earlier when hundreds of its advocates came together in Washington, D.C., to lobby for the group's cause. In coordination with other NGOs, including Resolve Uganda and the Enough Project, Invisible Children's supporters met for its "Lobby Days," when its young backers protested together and then swarmed out across the capital to lobby members of Congress.[18] Its supporters had also been able to mobilize in states and congressional districts and, most notably, had camped out in an eleven-day "sleep out" outside of Senator Tom Coburn's (R–Okla.) Oklahoma City office after he raised concern over financing the LRA disarmament bill.[19] After that, some members of Congress feared being "Coburned" or became more comfortable supporting the bill once Coburn agreed not to stand in its way.[20]

When discussing the reasons for supporting the bill to further address Joseph Kony's and the LRA's activities, many members of Congress pointed explicitly to the young people's lobbying. One of the bill's most ardent supporters in the House of Representatives, Ed Royce (R–Calif.), stated, "[That] this legislation has made it this far is really a tribute to a group of young people, young professionals, who have come up here on their own time and gone to universities around this country to organize in order to make people aware of the plight of these children in Africa."[21] Royce also wrote, "Frankly, without advocacy NGOs, this would be a forgotten conflict."[22]

Senator Russ Feingold similarly noted, "We have come a long way in just a few years, thanks especially to young Americans who have become increasingly aware of and outspoken about this horrific situation."[23] Speaking about his own political knowledge of Kony, Congressman Jerry Moran (R–Kans.) stated, "I was recently reminded of the severity of this situation when students in my hometown of Hays and the community of Sterling, Kansas, shared with me the latest news of this conflict."[24] Congresswoman Gwen Moore (D–Wisc.) added, "This legislation is also the result of the hard work of thousands of activists across the country—young and old—including from my district as well who want to ensure justice and peace for the many victims of the LRA."[25] House Foreign Affairs Committee chair Ilena Ros-Lehtinen (R–Fla.) stated similarly, "This topic is largely due to the tireless efforts of young advocates throughout the United States, including in my own congressional district, who have passionately taken up the cause of those whose lives have been destroyed by the LRA."[26] Congressman David Reichert (R–Wash.) noted in May 2010, "I learned about this legislation when four young people came into my district office last year to urge me to support H.R. 2478. I was—and still am—incredibly impressed with their passion and knowledge."[27]

This evidence suggests an active, well-organized foundation of support, which applied pressure on members of Congress in their home states as well as in Washington, D.C. Invisible Children was especially well organized in conservative-leaning states, which likely speaks to its ability to reach conservative members of Congress. Perhaps events such as the targeted lobbying of Senator Coburn also produced disincentives to oppose the bill to disarm the LRA, knowing that a protest outside of a congressional district office would generate unwanted political and media attention. Electoral pressures are not the only factor involved in explaining why this legislation passed, but a solid body of evidence suggests that this NGO activism, which included political lobbying from constituents in members' districts and states, "contributed overwhelmingly to the passage of [the Lord's Resistance Army Disarmament and Northern Uganda Recovery] Act [of 2009]."[28]

Personal Policy Preferences

It is very difficult analytically to separate the influence of constituency pressures on a member of Congress from the member's personal policy preferences. For example, a sustained liberal voting record on human rights might simply be a reflection of a member's district or state constituency demands and not necessarily of a member's deep ideological commitment to the advancement of human rights. What, however, seems evident in the LRA case is certain members' consistent and extended interest in capturing Joseph Kony. In the examples discussed in this section, these members' legislative activism involved long-term lobbying efforts for which there were far fewer electoral rewards. The members discussed here went beyond simple co-sponsorship of the legislation, which allows a member of Congress simply to claim credit for a bill's legislative success, and actually did the legislative work necessary to ensure its passage, which can be viewed as a measure of their personal policy preferences.

The original co-sponsor of the legislation was Wisconsin senator Russ Feingold, who had served on the Senate Foreign Relations Subcommittee on African Affairs and had a long-standing interest in the protection of human rights. In this sense, his efforts to push Congress squared closely with his voting patterns and personal ideology, which placed him solidly within the political left favorable to human rights concerns.[29] Feingold was the lead voice in calling for the United States to do more to address the atrocities Kony and the LRA committed.[30] In one of his addresses, he noted that he had "visited the displacement camps in northern Uganda and saw first-hand the impact the violence orchestrated by the LRA has had throughout the region."[31] After his 2007 visit to Uganda, Feingold returned to the United States with a heightened interest in addressing the atrocities caused by the LRA.[32] Moreover, the issue had some personal family appeal: he noted that his own daughters had helped educate him about Joseph Kony.[33] Feingold and his staff were also closely involved in the legislative process to advance the bill's prospects of being passed, which included lobbying other senators and congressmen. When Senator Tom Coburn raised opposition over funding the bill, Feingold's staff worked closely with Coburn's to craft a legislative proposal in a manner that was more acceptable to Coburn.[34]

In addition to Feingold, Jim Inhofe (R–Okla.) was a strong supporter of this legislation. A mix of personal religious motivations, a personal dislike of Joseph Kony, and his own perceived expertise on Africa help explain Inhofe's interest in this issue. Inhofe was first encouraged to become engaged in African issues by Doug Coe, whom, Inhofe notes, "talked me into going to Africa, I had no interest in going to Africa."[35] Doug Coe, an evangelical Christian, serves as spiritual advisor to and directs the Fellowship Foundation, which oversees the annual National Prayer Breakfast. In addition, the foundation oversees a residence in Washington, D.C., where members of Congress meet and some reside. Among its supporters is Senator Inhofe.[36] The evidence of the extent to which Inhofe's personal religious identity shapes his foreign-policy interest in Africa seems quite clear. Inhofe notes, "I'm guilty of two things. . . . I'm a Jesus guy, and I have a heart for Africa."[37] With strong evangelical tones, Inhofe stated in 2002, "I'm planning to meet with nine presidents in Abidjan, Cote d'Ivoire. My focus here will be to meet in the spirit of Jesus."[38]

Since the onset of his interest in Africa, Inhofe has traveled often to Africa, which has led him to argue that "I know Africa better than anyone else certainly in the United States Senate."[39] Thus, due to his personal religious identification with African issues, coupled with his own personal knowledge of Africa and the LRA, he has pushed aggressively for Kony's capture.[40] NGOs that actively supported this legislation identified Inhofe as a key supporter of capturing Kony. In addition, he also actively lobbied Senator Tom Coburn to vote for the legislation.[41] Thus, like Feingold, Inhofe demonstrated a sustained interest in capturing Kony and made independent political initiatives to help the LRA bill move forward.

Along with Russ Feingold, Senator Sam Brownback (R–Kans.) served as sponsor of the initial bill, and, also like Feingold, he served on the Senate's Foreign Relations Subcommittee on African Affairs, though his main interest in humanitarian affairs appears to stem from his bout with cancer in the mid-1990s. With an uncertain health prognosis, he awoke one night with existential questions and fears and determined that too much of his life was centered on personal ambition and not enough toward the concerns of others. This event prompted the conservative Republican to increasingly become a "bleeding heart conservative" with a greater interest in Africa. Recruited by Feingold to co-sponsor the legislation, Brownback noted that he is "pro-life and whole life" and took on a much greater interest in Africa.[42] Like Inhofe, he was also active in the Fellowship Foundation and in this sense shared similar religious convictions. Brownback was not the face of this legislation, but certainly this co-sponsorship from a Republican noted for his socially conservative perspective brought immediate bipartisan appeal to this legislation and again seemed to center around his personal humanitarian and evangelical interest in African issues.[43]

In the House of Representatives, three members served as original co-sponsors of the legislation: Jim McGovern (D–Mass.), Ed Royce (R–Calif.), and Brad Miller (D–N.C.). McGovern was a strong advocate for the legislation, which fit closely with his ideological policy preferences. He had "a solid liberal voting record" and served as the co-chair of Congress's Human Rights Caucus.[44] He was thus an important ally for the cause in the House, working closely with Senator Feingold's staff to advance the legislation.[45]

Congressman Royce, like Senator Feingold, had also long expressed concern over the human rights violations in Africa and had demonstrated a sustained interest in the atrocities committed by Joseph Kony and the LRA.[46] Though Royce has admitted on a number of occasions the significance of NGO pressure in raising awareness of this issue, it is also evident that he played a leadership role in advancing the issue to his congressional colleagues. In 2009, he took the additional step of lobbying with actress Kristen Hill, who came to Washington to work with Royce to gain additional co-sponsors of this legislation.[47] Through this effort and other lobbying efforts, Royce was viewed as an important ally to the advocacy NGOs not only because of his commitment to the cause but also because as a Republican he immediately brought bipartisan support to the issue.[48] Royce also forged a close relationship with the founders of Invisible Children and has continued to advance their cause.[49] In addition, Royce's staff worked closely with Senator Feingold's staff to ensure the successful passage of this legislation.[50] Although a researcher can never speak with certainty regarding a politician's personal motivations, there is evidence of these congressional members' ongoing and sustained interest in capturing Kony.

Partisanship

Despite what much of the research on congressional foreign-policy behavior and partisanship suggests, the legislative process for this bill was largely devoid of partisan politics. A number of factors help explain why this legislation was so bipartisan. First, from the time the bill was introduced, as indicated earlier, it had bipartisan cooperation, with original co-sponsors from both parties. In the Senate, Russ Feingold and Sam Brownback introduced the legislation; in the House, James McGovern, Ed Royce, and Brad Miller served as the original co-sponsors. Though a number of studies point to a Congress that has become increasingly partisan in the post–Cold War era, others maintain that a degree of bipartisanship still remains on African issues.[51] Both Brownback and Feingold served on the Senate Foreign Relations Subcommittee on African Affairs and thus formed an early partnership on this issue that conferred an immediate bipartisan identity to the bill, especially given that these two senators often opposed each other across an array of other issues. Eventually 65 senators and 202 representatives signed on as co-sponsors. In the Senate, 46 Democrats served as co-sponsors compared to 19 Republicans, which included Senate majority leader Harry Reid (D–Nev.), majority whip Richard Durbin (D–Ill.), and Foreign Relations Committee chair John Kerry (D–Mass.). In the House, 142 Democrats were co-sponsors along with 60 Republicans.[52] By this count, some partisan politics is evident, with Democrats more likely to serve as co-sponsors, though in an era of intense partisan congressional dynamics the number of co-sponsors from both parties suggests strong bipartisan backing. In fact, the only meaningful opposition to the legislation came from Senator Tom Coburn, but his opposition was based primarily on the financing of a new strategy.[53] Once he became more comfortable with the legislation's fiscal aspects and perhaps in light of the intense negative publicity that his opposition garnered in his home state, that opposition faded. No other members of Congress raised significant political stands against the bill.

Another political factor that helped remove partisanship from the debate was Joseph Kony's status in the United States as a terrorist. In 2001, President George W. Bush had placed Joseph Kony and the LRA on the U.S. Terror Exclusion List, which identified groups and individuals that the United States sought to bar from entry into the United States.[54] In 2008, the State Department also identified Kony as a "Specially Designated Global Terrorist."[55] Few issues unify Americans more than their nearly uniform disdain for "terrorists." National polls taken in 2009 and 2010 still indicated that terrorism topped Americans' list of perceived threats. In 2009, when the Kony legislation was first introduced, 59 percent of Americans indicated that terrorism was their top international concern.[56] Similar levels of public concern for terrorism extended into 2010 even in comparison to a range of perceived domestic threats.[57] Thus, many members of the House went to the floor to note their support for the LRA disarmament bill due to Kony's status as a human rights abuser who targeted children and as a terrorist. For example, Ed Royce noted that Kony was "perhaps the most wanted man in Africa. He is an indicted war criminal. He is a designated terrorist."[58] Congressman Eliot Engel (D–N.J.) noted that the legislation was intended to end the "LRA's reign of terror."[59] Congressman Chris Van Hollen (D–Md.) similarly added that "the LRA is currently branded a terrorist organization by the U.S. Government."[60] Even though the LRA's threat to Americans was essentially nonexistent, a number of members chose to use the language of terrorism to justify their support for the bill, which helped them to reach a broad congressional constituency and thus increased the attractiveness of going after Kony.

Another factor that may have spurred support for the proposed legislation was its ostensible natural policy evolution, which in very basic terms simply called upon the president to develop a new strategy to capture Kony and other LRA leadership. Such a step followed suit with previous actions in the George W. Bush administration. In 2008, Bush had authorized Operation Lightning Thunder, in which approximately seventeen "advisors and analysts" from the U.S. Department of Defense's African Command worked with the Ugandan military to wage a military offensive against the LRA. The mission failed and likely resulted in a counteroffensive by the LRA that killed some nine hundred civilians.[61] Thus, the call for a new strategy after this failed operation, coupled with Kony's status as an indicted war criminal, terrorist, and human rights violator of children, was not a radical policy development for the United States.[62]

In the same vein, the ambiguity of the newly proposed legislation did not necessarily commit a member of Congress to anything specific. Congress was simply calling for a new strategy.[63] The bill's actual "statement of policy" section proposed that the United States assist regional African governments by "providing political, economic, military, and intelligence support for viable multilateral efforts to protect civilians from the Lord's Resistance Army, to apprehend or remove Joseph Kony and his top commanders from the battlefield in the continued absence of a negotiated solution, and to disarm and demobilize the remaining Lord's Resistance Army Fighters."[64] In this regard, Congress essentially built into the bill an abdication of decision-making authority and asked the president to solve the problem through whatever means he, rather than Congress, thought best. This approach provided political benefits to members of Congress: if the president developed a strategy that members of Congress later opposed, those members could argue that the legislation never intended for the president to take such an action. Although Senator Feingold argued that the president was not authorized to use force abroad, the bill clearly provided much discretion to the president, including explicitly military solutions.

Moreover, another aspect of this ambiguous legislation that likely helped eliminate partisan attack is the manner in which members voted. In the Senate, the unanimous-consent procedure was used. It is commonly utilized to pass legislation, especially when the number of co-sponsors is high, yet it does not require each member of Congress to record a vote in favor of or opposition to the bill in question and in this sense provides some political protection against future developments that may not square with a member's electoral, partisan, or personal preferences. The House of Representatives similarly used a voice-vote procedure on the bill rather than an actual recorded vote, which again protects members of Congress from a policy direction gone sour. In addition, a member who is not comfortable with specific legislation but at the same time does not wish to openly oppose it can simply abstain from involvement. Thus, when the actual LRA bills were brought to the Senate and House floors, no voices of opposition were raised. The bills were quickly introduced and then quickly advanced.[65] Thus, again there is evidence in this case that Congress avoided political responsibility for the mission, an avoidance that could occur in part because of a legislative process that allowed members of Congress to distance themselves from the policy in the event that the president's actions became politically unpopular.

When President Obama announced his decision to send one hundred troops to Africa to carry out the legislation, Republican opposition to his actions reached its political apex, though it was still quite contained. One of his most immediate critics was conservative radio talk-show personality Rush Limbaugh, who argued that Joseph Kony and the LRA were Christians who were doing good by warring with Muslims in South Sudan. When confronted with information regarding Kony's human rights record, Limbaugh added that he would do more research on the issue.[66]

Another critic, Republican presidential candidate Congresswoman

Michele Bachmann (R–Minn.), noted, "I don't think that we should have gone in—I don't think the president should have committed those troops in Uganda," even though she had asserted no voice when the actual legislation was being debated and up for a vote.[67] Senator John McCain (R–Ariz.), one of the subjects of the next chapter, has nearly always argued for a commander in chief with unlimited constitutional powers to determine when and how American forces are used abroad. But in this case he stated, "I'm very disappointed, again, that the administration is not consulted [sic] with members of Congress before taking such action."[68] With the exception of Senator Coburn's earlier fiscal concerns, almost all opposition to any policy development related to Joseph Kony came *after* President Obama's announcement. The originally introduced legislation allowed the bill to move forward without meaningful or partisan opposition but also invited possible complaints once the president announced what the strategy would be, which is precisely what happened in this case. Thus, for a number of reasons, including the bill's bipartisan identification from the onset, the variety of nonpartisan reasons for confronting Joseph Kony, as well as the legislative process that built in congressional deference to the president, the bill experienced very little partisanship or congressional responsibility for possible military action to come.

NGO Activity and Political Access

The final political element of this case, which is not directly captured by the research on congressional members' electoral benefits, personal policy preferences, and partisan behavior or by the notion of congressional deference, is the specific roles played by NGOs in the legislative process. In this case, as in previous cases of human rights legislation, the role of a former NGO staffer who later became a governmental employee, Peter Quaranto from Resolve Uganda, appears to have had some relevance in the legislative process.[69]

Resolve Uganda was founded in 2007 after three university students, including Peter Quaranto, took study abroad trips to Uganda and learned more about the atrocities committed by the LRA. Like Invisible Children, Resolve is for the most part devoted to addressing human rights abuse in Uganda and ending the atrocities committed by Joseph Kony. It is important to consider for a number of reasons. First, after working for a year to help found Resolve, in August 2008 Quaranto took a position as a legislative assistant to Senator Russ Feingold, the LRA disarmament bill's original sponsor. By a number of accounts, Feingold's staff was critical in generating political support for the bill from senators and their staffs. Resolve co-founder and Quaranto's former colleague Michael Poffenberger noted that it was "helpful" to have Quaranto in Feingold's office.[70] A former government relations associate with the Enough Project, another NGO closely involved in the legislation, similarly noted that Quaranto was one of the "main individuals" she worked with in advancing the legislation.[71] In this respect, the NGO movement had an in-house advocate for the cause, who shared Senator Feingold's as well as these NGOs' passion for this legislation. Feingold's staff also actively courted Resolve's and Enough's policy expertise and insights on the actual legislation. This practice was common for Senator Feingold's office, which reached out to NGOs for their input.[72] Thus, some degree of political symbiosis was present in this legislation as Resolve Uganda, the Enough Project, and Feingold's office worked closely to advance the bill. Though it cannot be concluded that Quaranto's presence in Feingold's office was essential to the bill's passage, it is clear that a deeply committed individual employed by Feingold worked with his former NGO colleagues as well as with other Senate staffers to help pass this legislation.

Apart from the political access provided to NGOs in this case, a high degree of NGO coordination between Invisible Children, Resolve Uganda, and the Enough Project helped to consolidate the political pressure that could be placed on Congress. These three groups served as co-sponsors of the Lobby Days protests, which brought supporters of the bill to Washington, D.C., to rally for the cause and to lobby members of Congress. In addition, each NGO had unique political skills. Invisible Children was critical in generating widespread grassroots support for the cause and essential in building a national movement. Resolve Uganda understood Washington politics well and used its legislative expertise to help advance the issue within Washington. The Enough Project worked with the other two groups, and its director, John Prendergast, was able to generate various kinds of media attention to the issue. He was active in highlighting the LRA's human rights abuses, which by some accounts served a "legitimizing" function in the cause, given Prendergast's public media presence.[73] In sum, NGO access to Senate staff and their coordinated political pressure are important components of this bill's legislative history.

President Obama's decision to send one hundred U.S. troops to Central Africa was prompted by Congress members' actions. Congress thus played an active part in shaping the decision to utilize the U.S. military abroad. This mission continued through 2013 because Kony remained elusive, though considerable pressure had been placed on the LRA and Kony's subordinate leaders due to U.S. military assistance.[74] The findings in this chapter support some of the previous literature on Congress's role in foreign policy and at the same time build on the existing literature regarding congressional deference to the commander in chief.

Members of Congress can be motivated by their constituents to take action. As demonstrated here, the political pressure implemented by the NGO Invisible Children was considerable across a number of congressional districts. This movement was especially well organized in politically conservative regions of the United States, which likely helped conservative members of Congress respond more favorably to an issue that they would generally view as a traditional liberal human rights concern. This case also found evidence that members of Congress will work hard to advance issues that have especially strong personal appeal for them. Senator Feingold and Congressman Royce fit this characterization especially well. This issue also entailed a Christian evangelical element in that members of Congress who see their roles in an evangelical spirit felt a special responsibility to address the atrocities committed by Joseph Kony. It was, however, largely devoid of partisan politics, in part because the human rights violations involved atrocities committed against children but also in part because of Joseph Kony's status as a terrorist, which in many respects is a nonpartisan issue for Americans. Moreover, the legislative tools employed to pass this bill as well as its ambiguity provide important insight on how it was passed. Another important variable in this case was political access: NGOs coordinated their lobbying activities and had strong advocates for this issue within the Congress, who worked hard to advance the legislation.

Although one may conclude that a "perfect storm" of political variables came together to help pass this legislation—including constituency pressure, terrorism, violations of children's human rights, bipartisanship, congressional deference, and deeply committed members of Congress, as well as evangelical elements present in the Congress and in the grassroots movement—Invisible Children was critical in setting a political grassroots foundation in place. Years of advocacy, combined with these political forces, helped to generate congressional support for this issue, resulting in the deployment of U.S. military personnel to Central Africa.

6

Senators Kerry and McCain

Empowering the Commanders in Chief

Across each of the four cases examined so far, albeit in different degrees, senior members of Congress, including party leaders and committee chairpersons, worked to empower the commander in chief while generally insulating rank-and-file members of Congress from legislative and constitutional responsibility for the president's military actions abroad. As demonstrated in chapter 4 especially, John Kerry (D–Mass.) and John McCain (R–Ariz.) played leading roles in the Senate in protecting President Obama from legislative efforts to limit the commander in chief's bombings in Libya. In coming to the president's defense, Kerry criticized those who sought to invoke the WPR, siding closely with the Obama administration's view that the United States was not engaged in hostilities in Libya. McCain chastised members of the House for raising constitutional challenges to the commander in chief and called for *more* aggressive military action against Qaddafi. Kerry, then the chairman of the Senate Foreign Relations Committee, and McCain, then the ranking minority member of the Senate Armed Services Committee, sought to exercise influence and leadership on war powers by shaping the debate and limiting Congress's oversight role.

This chapter takes a different approach by examining the records of two senators in particular over their congressional careers. Both senators are Vietnam War veterans and since their first congressional elections have focused much of their policy attention on foreign and military affairs. Each senator has also clearly sought leadership roles in his respective caucus, and both were unsuccessful presidential candidates. Though it is difficult to measure the precise degree of influence Kerry and McCain exercised among their colleagues in the Senate at various points, what is clear is that both have long records of supporting the commander in chief regardless of his party affiliation. Though they ostensibly share different views on the WPR, it is politically significant that these two senior senators have nearly always sided with the commander in chief when he chose to use force abroad and when he made claims for essentially unilateral constitutional authority to wage war. Assessing their views and actions over a number of presidencies provides greater insight on the war powers interplay during the Obama administration and helps explains how and why Congress has so often abdicated its constitutional ability to check the commander in chief.

John Kerry and War Powers

A decorated veteran, John Kerry first gained national prominence as an articulate and outspoken critic of the U.S. military presence in Vietnam.[1] In 1971, he was invited to testify at a meeting of the Senate Foreign Relations Committee, chaired at the time by Senator J. William Fulbright (D–Ark.). In his recorded testimony and in an appeal to end U.S. participation in the war, Kerry advanced a number of basic constitutional principles on war powers, noting, "We are asking here in Washington for some action, action from the Congress of the United States of America which has the power to raise and maintain armies, and which by the Constitution also has the power to declare war."[2] In the statement, Kerry clearly referenced Congress's explicit war powers and called for Congress to exercise those powers.

Another indication of Kerry's rhetorical backing of Congress's war powers is his long-standing support of the WPR. During his Senate career, he frequently celebrated his support for the resolution. In 1986, upon the death of former senator Jacob Javits (R–N.Y.), who was the WPR's principal author, Kerry specifically lauded Javits's "intellectual and substantive

contribution to the issues of war and peace" and for "playing a constructive and positive role on" these issues.[3] In 1990, he also stated, "I am a
strong supporter and advocate of the War Powers Resolution,"[4] and again
expressed similar views in 1994.[5] On a number of occasions, Kerry, unlike
other members of Congress who have openly opposed the WPR, consis-
tently stated his adamant support for it. Based on this record, one may
conclude that during his time as a senator Kerry was a vigorous champion
of Congress's constitutional war powers and the WPR. Nearly all of the
evidence suggests otherwise, however.

Kerry and President Ronald Reagan's and George H. W. Bush's Military Actions

Kerry was first elected to the Senate to represent Massachusetts in 1984.
President Reagan was the first commander in chief he was required to
check and balance. During Kerry's early years in the Senate, both President Ronald Reagan and President George H. W. Bush carried out a
number of military actions in which Congress had limited, if any, input
on use-of-force decisions.

Prior to Kerry's election in 1983, President Reagan had deployed
approximately 8,000 American troops to Grenada, an invasion triggered by
the assassination of Grenadine leader Maurice Bishop, who had achieved
power through a coup d'état in 1979. Bishop had been friendly with Cuba
and the Soviet Union, but the rebel challenger, Bernard Coard, expressed
much more sympathy toward the communist allies, using boisterous anti-
American rhetoric along the way. In the broader policy context, the U.S.
troop deployment also matched closely the Reagan administration's desire
to "roll back" communism. Moreover, when the invasion occurred, Reagan officials also maintained that American medical students attend-
ing St. George's Medical College were threatened by Coard's rebellion,
although considerable doubt has been expressed regarding how threatened the students really were.[6]

According to key Reagan administration officials, Congress had no
role in the decision to use force in this case. George Shultz, secretary of
state at that time, wrote later that the Reagan foreign-policy principals
made the decision to strike, and then Shultz asked his staff to invite congressional leaders to the White House so that they could be informed of the
forthcoming military action.[7] As noted earlier, analysts have doubted the

degree to which Grenada represented an emergency and national-security threat to the United States, although a case can be made that the Reagan administration did take a number of diplomatic steps to avoid the use of force.[8] Moreover, eighteen Americans were killed in the operation, so by definition U.S. troops faced hostilities, one of the conditions outlined in the WPR. Key congressional leaders were notified about the forthcoming strike, but the decision to use force was made prior to any actual meeting with Congress; no consultation occurred, as the WPR requires.[9] Despite these well-known and generally uncontroversial facts, especially in the aftermath of the deployment, in 1993 Kerry noted his support for President Reagan's military action in Grenada,[10] which is notable considering such an egregious violation of the WPR and Kerry's previously stated support for the WPR and Congress's additional war powers. His support for Reagan's military operations did not end with Grenada, however.

In 1986, in the first major military action by an American president during Kerry's first Senate term, the Reagan administration conducted air strikes on Libyan leader Muammar Qaddafi. According to Reagan, the Libyan government was directly responsible for a terrorist strike on a German dance club frequented by American servicemen and -women. In addition to more than one hundred Germans, one U.S. soldier and sixty other Americans were wounded in the terrorist attack.[11]

As with Grenada, Congress had no decision-making role in the strikes on Libya. Members of Congress who had received prior notification of the forthcoming strikes admitted that they had no real ability to shape the actual decision to use force because Reagan administration officials notified congressional leaders only three hours before the military strikes on Qaddafi took place.[12] At the time, Senator Kerry, like most members of Congress, expressed no constitutional qualms about President Reagan's actions, as indicated in the *Congressional Record*. Ironically, the strikes on Qaddafi came less than one month after Kerry had lauded Senator Javits's career and the WPR.

As in his stance regarding the strikes on Grenada and Libya, Kerry also supported President George H. W. Bush in 1989 when Bush used 14,000 American troops to capture Panamanian leader Manuel Noriega in Operation Just Cause. Following the pattern established by Reagan, Bush informed congressional leaders of the forthcoming strikes only a few hours in advance. Four years later, in 1993, Kerry noted that "we made the right decision when we went into Grenada and into Panama, even though we knew casualties were a possibility."[13] In effect, he again supported a decision by the president that relegated Congress to a nonplayer in the actual decision to strike even though he ostensibly understood that hostilities were expected and resulted from the action.[14]

With the war on drugs high on the political agenda in the first year of the George H. W. Bush administration and before the 1989 U.S. invasion of Panama, Kerry also pushed President Bush to think more broadly about multilateral means to combat drug traffickers. He encouraged Bush to consider the creation of a multilateral drug strike force that would work in partnership with Caribbean states.[15] Kerry was not specific about how the strike force would operate or what the U.S. role in such an organization would be. Whatever its makeup, however, it did not include a substantive role for Congress when military decisions would be required. Such an organization would ostensibly have been involved in air and maritime patrols and would have required expeditious military decisions from its participants. Although many Americans supported the U.S. efforts to address the growing drug problem, Kerry's proposal would have led to additional empowerment of the executive branch in military matters.

One of the few exceptions to Kerry's otherwise carte blanche support for presidential wars occurred when Congress was faced with the decision to go to war to liberate Kuwait from Saddam Hussein's military occupation in 1991. In this case, Kerry voted against the use of force. When casting his vote, he spoke about the need for Congress to stand up and oppose this military action.[16] By taking this position, Kerry exercised his constitutional powers to check the president and through this opposition could not be accused of deference to the president.

In the hours that followed the ensuing military strikes, however, Kerry quickly rallied behind President Bush, noting that we should "support the troops" and that the troops should "not have the rug pulled out underneath them, that they not somehow wind up with second guessing[,] which then puts them at greater peril."[17] It is certainly admirable that Kerry openly backed American forces in combat and wished that no harm come to them during this moment of crisis. At the same time, his statements imply that it would no longer be right for Congress to challenge the president's decision and that any "checking" of the president would be inappropriate during combat. Senators Fulbright and Javits did not hold such a view during the Vietnam War, nor did Kerry nearly twenty years earlier when he had testified in front of the Senate Foreign Relations Committee and specifically called upon Congress to speak out against President Nixon's military operations in Vietnam.

In addition, approximately two months after the initial strikes and the U.S. military victory against Iraq, Kerry stated that on August 2, 1990, he *had* voted to support military action against Iraq if necessary. He emphasized that the Democrats and Republicans who voted against the use of force in January 1991 had "immediately rallied around the country and troops and gave full support to our military effort."[18] Kerry's statement again suggests that his constitutionally protected right to check the president did not extend to the time when American troops were in combat. No "balancing" would take place during war; rather, he sought to associate himself with the commander in chief's actions and divorce himself from his previous vote to check the president.

Thus, in his first eight years in the Senate, serving alongside two presidents who conducted a number of military actions, Kerry generally supported a strong commander in chief, who essentially went unchecked by the Congress. The one exception was his vote in 1991 against Operation Desert Storm, but he immediately backed away from that vote once the operation began. Otherwise, Kerry supported both presidents and their broadly perceived military powers in situations when the United States faced no imminent threat and U.S. troops were engaged in combat. Kerry's record on the WPR thus represents almost a complete abdication of congressional power to the commander in chief. Moreover, it should be noted that Kerry did not try to distinguish between "war" and military operations short of war, a distinction that some members of Congress have used to justify their deference to the commander in chief. The operations in Grenada and Panama were not "limited" strikes and involved thousands of U.S. ground troops, who engaged in combat and experienced casualties. Although these operations were different from the one against Iraq in 1991, a semantic debate over whether these operations were actually "war" diverts from the central point that Congress was not involved in the decisions to wage combat. Kerry did also not shy away from expressing his views and in this sense advanced his own foreign-policy perspectives in an effort to shape U.S. foreign policy and Congress's role in the policy-making process. It is also important to see that Kerry, a Democrat, largely supported two Republican administrations in their uses of force, which suggests his rally-around-the-flag deference despite his membership in the opposing party.

Kerry and President Clinton's Military Actions

Bill Clinton used force in a number of military operations during his presidency. Kerry did not always go to the Senate floor with opinions on the constitutionality of Clinton's actions, but his recorded responses indicate a clear trend. In each case, Kerry supported military action. In some cases, despite his previous support for the WPR, he took steps to ensure that Clinton would not be checked or limited by the Congress prior to a forthcoming military action.

In October 1993, after President Clinton's first major military crisis in Somalia, a number of Senate Republicans, led by Senator Don Nickles (R–Okla.), proposed an amendment to require congressional approval prior to U.S. troop involvement in UN-sponsored operations. Although the partisan rhetoric appeared high at the time, Nickles's proposal squared with the legislative history of the UN Participation Act of 1945. As established in chapter 1, this act maintained that U.S. troops could not participate in UN-sponsored military operations without the U.S. Congress's approval. Kerry responded to these Republican efforts by defending presidential freedom of action that provided wide discretion to the president, noting that "when you look hard at the Nickles amendment, it is clear that it does not deal with the problem before us, but it is probably unconstitutional on its face, since it purports to take away the power of the Commander in Chief as a commander in chief who has the right to order troops to fight in certain ways at certain times with certain people."[19] Although Kerry had previously noted his support for Congress's war powers, it is difficult to determine according to this statement under what conditions Congress *can* limit presidential military ambitions. Kerry here advanced an idea that provides much leeway to the commander in chief.

Similarly, Kerry went to great lengths to protect President Clinton prior to the deployment of 10,000 American troops to Haiti to restore President Jean Bertrand Aristide to power. Although the deployment was conducted after a negotiated settlement, it seemed reasonable, given the widespread political violence that had taken place since Aristide's ousting, to anticipate at the time that American troops would potentially face

"hostilities," a condition specified by the WPR for Congress to participate in decisions on whether to use force. Thus, it is little surprise that
American troops stepped onto Haitian soil armed and ready for combat.
Prior to the deployment, many Senate Republicans favored a vote on President Clinton's authority to use troops abroad in this operation, but senior
Democrats, led by majority leader George Mitchell (D–Me.), prevented a
vote from occurring.[20] Although siding with the senior Democrats, Kerry
stated, "I would prefer to have a vote. It is consistent with everything I
have ever said since I fought in Vietnam." Yet he also defended Clinton's
authority to deploy the troops, noting that the president sometimes faces
"the lonely decision" as commander in chief and that "there are times
when the buck stops at the desk of the President of the United States[,]
who has to make a decision."[21] Again, it is difficult to reconcile his previously stated ostensible support for the WPR and Congress's constitutional
war powers with his justification at this time for such wide powers for the
commander in chief.

Kerry similarly backed the president and the use of force when Clinton took military action in Bosnia and Kosovo through NATO.[22] In each
case, Congress took no binding decisions against the president prior to the
strikes, even though it was clear to most observers in the immediate days
before the strikes that military action was forthcoming.

On Clinton's multiple air and missile strikes against Iraq, it is difficult
to find a more ardent supporter of military action against Saddam Hussein and presidential war powers than Kerry. In September 1996, when
President Clinton fired forty-three cruise missiles on Iraq in response
to Hussein's strikes against Iranian-backed Kurdish resistance forces in
northern Iraq, no member of Congress was consulted prior to the strike.[23]
Kerry expressed no constitutional qualms or concerns about violations of
the WPR and instead argued, "President Clinton's response to Saddam's
latest challenge was the right one—decisive, measured, and carefully cal-
culated to take the strategic advantage away from Saddam."[24] In February 1998, when Clinton faced another crisis over Iraq's unwillingness to
comply with the UN weapons inspectors, Kerry suggested that he was
ready to use ground troops if necessary and noted that a strategic bombing would not likely be sufficient to deal with Hussein because it would
not remove the root cause of the compliance problem.[25] Kerry also raised
no constitutional objections to Operation Desert Fox, the four-day mili-

tary operation against Hussein in December 1998 that came without a specific congressional authorization to use force, nor did he challenge the president's authority to use force against Iraq for violations of the U.S.-imposed no-fly zones over northern and southern Iraq. Approximately 130 different strikes were conducted after Operation Desert Fox during the Clinton administration. Although President Clinton as well as many members of Congress claimed that Congress had previously authorized such military action with legislation in 1991, these claims suggest a rather broad interpretation of Congress's vote in 1991 to mean that it permitted perpetual authority to bomb Iraq, which the legislation did not provide.[26]

Kerry's choices and public positions on war powers with regard to many of Clinton's military actions were like those of most members of Congress, who rarely questioned Clinton's proclaimed authority to use force.[27] What makes Kerry stand out among members of Congress is the degree to which he defended Clinton's asserted powers as commander in chief, especially in those military operations conducted with UN approval. It is difficult to reconcile such views, however, with Kerry's earlier stated support for the WPR and for the importance of congressional war powers.

Kerry and President George W. Bush's Military Actions

President George W. Bush's two major military endeavors were in Afghanistan and Iraq. In both cases, as noted briefly in chapter 1, Congress was closely involved in writing the resolution language that permitted eventual military action. In both cases, Kerry played a leading role in shaping the political process that led to the use of force, which granted President Bush wide authority to conduct the military operations.

When Senate Joint Resolution 23, Authorization for Use of Military Force, came to the Senate floor on September 14, 2001, after the September 11 terrorist attacks, it was clear that negotiations and compromise had taken place between the White House and Congress. Senator Robert Byrd (D–W.Va.) noted that the president had initially requested unlimited spending powers in conducting the global war on terrorism, which Congress did not grant.[28] Senator Carl Levin (D–Mich.) added that the key negotiators had demanded that some reference be made to the WPR, which was included in the final resolution.[29] Bush officials also initially sought military authority to strike preemptively against terrorists, which

Congress opposed. Instead, congressional negotiators permitted the president to "prevent" acts of terrorism but not to strike preemptively, a decision that Congress viewed as a restraint on presidential powers.[30] In this respect, Congress clearly played some checking role toward the commander in chief, and Senator Kerry was a key participant in the negotiation process with the White House. The Congress thus turned back requests that would have grossly expanded presidential powers.

At the same time, however, a legitimate argument can be made that a great deal of legislative deference was embedded in the resolution itself. The key part of the Authorization for Use of Military Force (Public Law 107-40) reads: "That the President is authorized to use all necessary and appropriate force against those nations, organizations, or persons he determines planned, authorized, committed, or aided the terrorist attacks that occurred on September 11, 2001, or harbored such organizations or persons, in order to prevent any future acts of international terrorism against the United States by such organizations or persons" (sec. 2[a]). Such language permits extremely wide decision-making authority and military freedom in fighting the war on terrorism. Yet Senator Kerry nevertheless noted about the resolution that "it does not give the President a blanket approval to take military action against others under the guise of fighting international terrorism. It is not an open-ended authorization to use force in circumstances beyond those we face today."[31] Despite this ostensibly genuine view of the resolution, it is difficult to see how Congress had limited the president and what role, if any, Congress would play in the conduct of the war to come if the president argued that he was acting against terrorist threats according to the resolution's mandates.[32]

Moreover, additional evidence suggests that when the resolution was being negotiated, Senate Democrats broke from the House Democrats, who were demanding greater oversight and more intelligence sharing and who sought greater consultation before military action could occur. Differences still remained between the White House and the Democratic negotiators on September 13, when both sides parted. Yet the following day Senate majority leader Tom Daschle (D–S.D.) allowed the resolution to move forward in its current form to the Senate floor, where it passed unanimously. Clearly, the Senate favored a less involved role for Congress in fighting terrorists than the House did.[33]

Thus, although it is accurate to say that Congress played some checking role against the president initially in their discussions on aspects of the resolution's language, it also is fair to conclude that Congress granted wide discretion to the commander in chief in determining the conduct of the war on terrorism. Kerry, as a key negotiator on the Senate's behalf, was involved in the resolution language and so must be credited with granting wide authority to the commander in chief.

On Iraq, unlike on nearly all previous military actions conducted during his Senate tenure, Kerry played an instrumental role in calling for President Bush to gain congressional authorization prior to the actual use of force. In an op-ed article in the *New York Times,* he wrote that Bush "must seek advice and approval from Congress" before moving forward with military action on Saddam Hussein.[34] Despite Bush's claims in August 2002 of his existing authority to take military action against Iraq, the administration responded to Kerry and others' requests to seek congressional approval.[35] In this respect, Kerry and others effectively and publicly asserted their congressional war powers, which Bush eventually respected.

When House Joint Resolution 114, Authorization for Use of Military Force against Iraq Resolution of 2002 (October 11, 2001), eventually reached the Senate floor and was approved in a vote of 77 to 33, Kerry provided extensive remarks on it. He noted that the Congress had amended the president's original request to use military force across the Persian Gulf, instead limiting a military strike to Iraq. Kerry also noted that he had not voted for "regime change" but only to exercise military options in order to force Hussein to comply with the weapons inspectors. He also noted that Congress had won a victory by requesting that the president attempt to work through the UN rather than move forward without its consideration. Unlike Kerry's previous more deferential comments on U.S. military action, however, he noted that "we will hold them [the administration] accountable for the means by which we do this. . . . It is through constant questioning we will stay the course."[36]

As it did after September 11, 2001, Congress clearly provided some check on the president in this case and reined in the more wide-sweeping presidential claims of authority. Kerry was among the most public in calling for the president to gain congressional approval prior to the war, although in a book written several years later former senator Chuck Hagel (R–Neb.) does not identify Kerry among the Senate Democrats who played a key role in checking the president's requests but rather notes the efforts made by Senators Tom Daschle and Joe Biden (D–Del.) to tamp down the administration's wider ambitions.[37]

At the same time, the resolution still granted wide authority to the commander in chief in determining whether force would be used. Section 3(a) reads, "The President is authorized to use the Armed Forces of the United States as he determines to be necessary and appropriate." As discussed in chapter 1, some analysts make a legitimate argument that when making this vote for the resolution, Congress abdicated its war powers to the president, leaving it to the *commander in chief* rather than to Congress to make the final decision on war.[38]

Kerry later argued that he had been misled by the Bush administration and that the resolution he had voted for was not the policy that President Bush eventually adopted. In his presidential campaign in 2004, he argued that he had not voted for war with Iraq, but only to threaten war.[39] In some respects, he is correct, given that the resolution itself granted the president the authority to make the final determination for war. Nonetheless, virtually all observers understood that those who voted in 2002 to support the president, as Kerry did, were allowing the United States to move forward with war in Iraq. Moreover, even if this interpretation of Kerry's understanding of the vote on Iraq is incorrect, he expressed no constitutional qualms about the president's authority to use force when the war began. Nor did he join twelve members of the House of Representatives who filed suit against President Bush and Secretary of Defense Donald Rumsfeld in the U.S. District Court for the District of Massachusetts (ironically, Kerry's home state) for ignoring Congress's war powers authority *prior to* actual combat in Operation Iraqi Freedom.[40]

Thus, on Iraq, Kerry's record is again mixed. He and others members of Congress were fierce defenders of congressional war powers when the Bush administration attempted to move toward military action without congressional approval. He also suggested, seemingly for the first time, that he would hold the president accountable *during* war if necessary, which is a view that he had previously articulated at length in 1971. Yet he subsequently also voted for a resolution that gave wide military discretion to the commander in chief and was not among those who presented legal challenges to the president's authority to go to war.

As a leading foreign-policy voice in the Senate over the entirety of his career, Kerry clearly worked on many occasions to back the commander in chief in the vast majority of cases involving military action. In the two occasions when he played a leading role in checking the president, he later sought to distance himself from those votes. Thus, it is perhaps with little surprise that Kerry most recently played a prominent role in the U.S. Senate in protecting President Obama from congressional war powers checks over Libya and in leading the efforts in the Senate to argue that the United States was not involved in "hostilities" there. In sum, Kerry has a long history of *actively* working to limit Congress's war powers, making congressional interference in the president's war-fighting plans more difficult. In contrast to his long-standing rhetorical support for the WPR, his legislative actions demonstrate that although Congress is active, that activity in fact works to suppress legislative interference aimed against the commander in chief.

John McCain and War Powers

John McCain's legislative record with respect to Congress's war powers authority is different in substance from Kerry's and more mixed, though in many respects the result of his activity is the same: an empowered commander in chief. Like Kerry, McCain has often sought a foreign-policy leadership role in the Senate in matters shaping U.S. military actions abroad.

McCain first entered the Congress in 1983 after a successful run for a seat in the House of Representatives, representing the First Congressional District in Arizona. In 1986, he won a seat in the U.S. Senate, where he has remained since. Like John Kerry, McCain also ran two unsuccessful presidential campaigns, culminating in his 2008 nomination to run on the Republican presidential ticket against then senator Barack Obama.

While serving in the Congress, McCain has gravitated toward military and foreign-policy issues, a preference that, like John Kerry's, may stem in part from his status as a Vietnam veteran. McCain served as an aviator in the U.S. Navy. While on a mission in Vietnam in 1967, his aircraft was shot down, and he was captured by the North Vietnamese. He remained a prisoner of war until his release in 1973, after which he continued serving in the navy until 1981. McCain comes from a family with deep military ties; both his father and his grandfather were four-star admirals.

Though much research on both Kerry's and McCain's tenures in Congress points to an increasingly partisan Congress, with only a few exceptions McCain has often been a nonpartisan supporter of the commander in chief and for military action abroad. Like Kerry, he has always backed the commander in chief when the president seeks to use and deploy American forces. Although McCain has at times doubted the president's foreign- and military-policy decisions, he has nonetheless advanced a constitutional perspective that generally allows the president nearly unlimited power as commander in chief. In doing so, he has often helped thwart efforts within his own party to limit the commander in chief's asserted authority to use force and has played a leading role in backing the president in the lead-up to war. On rare occasions, McCain has called for a more effective WPR, but at other times he has criticized the act and its general intent of checking a commander in chief.

John McCain and President Ronald Reagan's Military Actions

The military actions conducted during Ronald Reagan's presidency provide useful perspectives on McCain's views on the constitutionality of military action abroad. Although his views on war powers were articulated more extensively during the Clinton and George W. Bush administrations, some early trends in his thinking are evident in his first years in Congress. The military actions and maneuvers in this early period include the 1982 deployment of U.S. armed forces to Lebanon in a multinational peacekeeping operation, the 1983 U.S. military strikes on Grenada, the strikes on Qaddafi in 1986, and the U.S. military protection of Kuwaiti oil tankers in 1987.

In the Reagan presidency, the first major war powers question for John McCain arose with the deployment of approximately eight hundred American armed forces to Beirut, Lebanon, in August 1982. At the time of the initial deployment, McCain was not yet a member of Congress. However, within his first year in office he shared his views on the WPR and war powers more generally. In October 1983, Congress forwarded House Joint Resolution 364, which provided statutory authorization under the WPR for continued U.S. participation in the multinational peacekeeping forces in Lebanon but placed an eighteen-month time limit on the operation.[41] Reagan indicated that he supported congressional action to approve of the operation and worked to find a compromise with members of Congress who had grown increasingly concerned with the U.S. deployment, but once the resolution passed, he stated his general opposition to any congressional mandate that would limit his own perceived power as commander in chief.[42]

In response to Democratic-led challenges, McCain opposed the resolution to limit the operation to eighteen months and the invocation of the WPR.[43] His comments on his vote are noteworthy and an early indicator of his preference for a strong commander in chief. "It is with great reluctance that I rise in opposition to this resolution," he said. "I am well known for my respect for the President of the United States and for supporting his policies. I do not believe the President should be restricted in fulfilling his constitutionally mandated responsibility of conducting our Nation's foreign policy."[44] This position provides an early indicator of his view to come: that the president should not be restricted as commander in chief.

McCain's view on war powers was tested again in the U.S. military invasion of Grenada in 1983. In the aftermath of the deployment, McCain supported House Joint Resolution 402, which declared that the WPR became operative on October 25, 1983—the initial day of the invasion—and that the president had sixty days to complete the military operation.[45] The House's vote, however, was not controversial and was approved 403 to 23.[46] In this respect, McCain's vote fell in line with nearly all members of Congress, who were also likely reacting to the suicide bombing in Lebanon on October 23, 1983, which resulted in the deaths of 241 American soldiers.

It is important to note that Congress had no role in the decision to use force in Grenada. The Reagan administration made its decision and then informed members of Congress of the military strikes to come.[47] On the House floor, McCain provided no comments on either the invasion or the decision-making process that led to the invasion. Yet later in 1988 and again in 1998, he voiced his support for these strikes and implicitly for the decision-making process that produced this military action.[48] In short, these first two military operations in 1983 provide an early and telling glimpse of McCain's views, which indicate his strong backing for a commander in chief who acted without seeking congressional input.

President Reagan also conducted military strikes in Libya in 1986, and once again, as noted earlier, Congress had no role in that decision either. In the aftermath of the strikes, McCain recorded no statement on the House floor regarding the strikes or on the decision-making process that resulted in the military action. Two years later, however, on the opening night of the 1988 Republican National Convention in New Orleans, he criticized the Democratic Party's nominee, Michael Dukakis, for opposing the bombings of Libya.[49] In doing so, McCain demonstrated his support for Reagan's military actions and, again, implicitly for the decision-making process that led to the strikes.

Additional military maneuvers that merit analysis include the various naval escort operations that took place in the Persian Gulf in 1987, when U.S. naval ships flagged and escorted Kuwaiti oil tankers in an effort to protect the tankers as they moved through the gulf. Now as a member of the U.S. Senate, McCain adamantly opposed any effort to trigger an invocation of the WPR, as Senators John Warner (R–Va.) and San Nunn (D–Ga.) were advocating.[50] In these debates, McCain dismissively referred to the WPR as the "retreat powers act."[51] On the question of whether Congress should take a policy stand before military action takes place, McCain remarked that "peace in the world cannot be legislated by congressional restrictions on the President's defense powers."[52] Thus, with regard to the Reagan administration's military actions, McCain's disdain for the WPR was evident, as was his view of a commander in chief who should have wide discretion in determining when force may be used abroad.

McCain and President George H. W. Bush's Military Actions

McCain continued to be a strong backer of presidential military action during George H. W. Bush's presidency. He did not speak extensively on the constitutionality of Bush's military actions, but his broader policy support for the commander in chief provides additional evidence of his views in favor of an empowered commander in chief.

Congress was out of session when the U.S. invasion of Panama occurred in 1989, which may partially explain the absence of any substantive discussion on the House or Senate floor regarding Bush's decision-making process or the mission itself. Like most others, McCain did not immediately register a statement in the *Congressional Record* in response to the military action. However, in later years he explicitly noted that "we were correct to liberate Grenada and Panama, despite the loss of life that accompanied those conflicts,"[53] and thus he implicitly expressed his support for Bush's military decision making that was devoid of congressional input.

Much like his position on Panama, McCain actively supported an empowered commander in chief to conduct military operations in Iraq during the 1991 Gulf War. In response to Saddam Hussein's decision to invade Kuwait on August 2, 1990, McCain was quick to demonstrate his disdain for Hussein's actions. He also stated that the only way we could "protect our friends, ourselves, and our values against men like Saddam Hussein" was to use "forceful action and military preparedness."[54] Once the war began, which McCain voted to support, he noted that the United States was the only country that could successfully "check Saddam's empire building [ambitions]."[55]

In 1999, reflecting on the debates in Congress that had led up to the authorization to use force in 1991, McCain indicated that Congress did a "model" job and had one of its "finest hours" in handling the situation that led up to the war.[56] At the same time, he did not object to the Bush administration's views that congressional authorization for the forthcoming war was not necessary before military action took place.

Thus, McCain supported both military strikes during George H. W. Bush's presidency and raised no qualms about Bush's constitutional assertions of an empowered commander in chief.

McCain and Bill Clinton's Military Actions

Among the different deployments and various military strikes made during the Clinton administration, one of the most instructive discussions of McCain's views on war powers took place prior to Clinton's troop deployment to Haiti in 1994. As the Clinton administration moved closer toward military action against Haiti's ruling junta, Senator Arlen Specter (R–Pa.) offered an amendment that called for the prohibition of a U.S. troop deployment to Haiti without specific congressional authorization. Specter included certain exceptions that permitted the president to act militarily if American citizens in Haiti needed immediate military protection or if U.S. national-security interests demanded immediate military action that precluded the opportunity to gain congressional authorization. Mostly, however, this amendment was aimed at restricting the president's ability to act militarily in Haiti without explicit congressional approval.[57]

As the chief opponent to this amendment among Specter's fellow Republicans, McCain provided an extended defense and articulation of his views on the Constitution and war powers. He first noted that he agreed with Specter that American troops should *not* be deployed to Haiti.[58] However, his qualm about the amendment was on the constitutional grounds that Specter's proposal "exceeds the authority of the Congress of the United States."[59] McCain maintained that "it is impossible for legislative bodies to anticipate world events. That is why our Founding Fathers put those responsibilities, enormous responsibilities—the lives of American service men and women—within the authority of the President of the United States."[60] As he had implied previously but in this case argued explicitly, he advocated a vision of a commander in chief with unilateral powers for determining when, where, and how U.S. military force may be used.

McCain further elaborated, noting that "at no time during those [Cold War] years would I have contemplated prohibiting the President of the United States from military actions any place in the world. . . . The fact is that the President of the United States is given the responsibility of sending into harms way our greatest national treasure, our young men and women."[61] McCain's perspective of war powers permitted Congress no role in the initial decision to use military force abroad. To make it even clearer, he added that Congress does not have "the right to declare peace,"[62] as he had similarly stated in 1987.

Specter rebutted that McCain's vision of presidential powers implied that Congress's constitutional right to declare war is then irrelevant—that the right to declare war had no constitutional bearing on McCain's vision of how force may be used.[63] McCain responded by noting that Congress does have the power of the purse to end a U.S. military mission, but otherwise Congress's war powers appeared to begin and end there.[64]

McCain took a similar position prior to the deployment of 20,000 American troops to the NATO peacekeeping mission in Bosnia in 1995, which had approval from the UN Security Council. In leading the Senate's discussion with Senate majority leader Robert Dole (R–Kans.), McCain noted, "I agree with those senators who have said that they would not have undertaken the commitment made by the President of the United States to deploy American ground forces to Bosnia to implement the tenuous peace that now exists there. But that is no longer the central question of our deliberations this evening. The President did so commit and our obligation now goes beyond expressing our disagreement with that decision. . . . Many of us did disagree. . . . Yet we all recognize that the President has the authority to make that decision."[65] Again, McCain, despite his opposition to the actual policy of deploying these forces to Bosnia, maintained that the Congress had no real authority to prevent the commander in chief from taking this action; such a view certainly runs counter to the congressional agreements reached for U.S. entry into the United Nations in 1945 and into NATO in 1949.

Another display of McCain's belief in a strong and unlimited president occurred during NATO's bombing campaign against Slobodan Milosevic's military and police forces in Yugoslavia in 1999. As the air strikes continued into the campaign's sixth week with little sign of political or strategic progress for NATO, McCain led an effort in the Senate to provide Clinton the ability to use "all necessary force"—which, by implication, would include the use of American ground forces if the president desired—to defeat Milosevic.[66] In describing his efforts to encourage the president to use force more aggressively, McCain noted: "I have said repeatedly that the President does not need this resolution to use all the force he deems necessary to achieve victory in Kosovo. I stand by that contention. And I have the good company of the Constitution behind me."[67] At the time, President Clinton opposed the "all necessary force" resolution, and McCain was critical of the Clinton administration's military approach, which excluded the use of ground forces. McCain's proposal was defeated, but it nonetheless provides another meaningful demonstration of the extent to which he felt that the commander in chief is permitted to use force abroad without constraint.[68] From McCain's perspective in these cases, presidents are free to initiate wars at their own discretion and in the manner they choose.

On President Clinton's many strikes against Iraq, McCain similarly supported the commander in chief. For example, in 1998 when a number of senators raised concerns over the timing of the Clinton administration's strikes against Iraq, which came on the eve of the House impeachment hearings, McCain aggressively backed Clinton, even though only a few members of Congress had been notified in advance of the forthcoming military action.[69]

In 1996, however, McCain uncharacteristically raised some concerns over the decision-making process prior to the strikes on Iraq. In this case, McCain voiced some unease over the Clinton administration's absence of consultation with Congress and suggested the need for a more effective WPR.[70] At this time, McCain was serving as an informal foreign-policy advisor in Robert Dole's presidential campaign and was rapidly becoming a lead Republican critic of the Clinton administration's foreign policy. McCain had been especially critical of Clinton's policy toward Iraq, maintaining that U.S. foreign policy had gone weak toward Hussein under Clinton.[71]

Moreover, in 1999 in an interview at the Center for Strategic and International Studies, McCain also noted that the WPR had been "routinely violated" across all administrations and that a need existed to "review and revise the War Powers Resolution so that it makes sense and we can abide by our own laws."[72] These two expressions of concern over the WPR contrast strongly with his earlier statements in the Reagan and Bush eras, when he raised no objections to violations of it, and are difficult to square with the constitutional perspectives he advanced regarding U.S. foreign policy toward Bosnia and Kosovo. McCain's calls for a more effective WPR in 1999 also contrast quite sharply with his criticisms of the resolution in 1987 and with his views in favor of an essentially independent commander in chief that he championed in 1994 prior to military action in Haiti. Although it is difficult to explain McCain's sudden (and limited) backing of the WPR, these outlier criticisms of Clinton may simply have been partisan critiques and in general do not reflect the more traditional claims of presidential military preeminence that McCain more frequently advanced.

Regarding other major military action during the Clinton presidency, the 1998 military strikes on suspected al-Qaeda posts in Afghanistan and Sudan, McCain again expressed his support for military action and raised no qualms regarding the decision-making process prior to the strikes.[73] Clinton administration officials had made some effort to consult key congressional leaders before the strikes took place, and thus a case can be made that some aspects of the WPR were more closely met in this case than for other previous military strikes abroad.[74] Nonetheless, McCain's support for this military action abroad fell in line with his long history of backing the commander in chief when the president determined that military action was necessary and appropriate. Thus, apart from his changes in tune in 1996 and 1999, McCain otherwise was a leading voice in the Senate during the Clinton years for a strong commander in chief and at times battled with his own political party to combat assertions of congressional war powers, which he deemed unconstitutional.

McCain and President George W. Bush's Military Actions

As in the pattern McCain had established in previous American military actions, he was instrumental in defending the resolutions to use force against al-Qaeda and Iraq in the administration of George W. Bush and fought against any limitations on the president's asserted war-making authority. On the resolution that permitted military action against al-Qaeda and anyone associated with the September 11 attacks on the United States (Senate Joint Resolution 23), McCain spoke forcefully in favor of military action. He again argued for a commander in chief with essentially unlimited powers in conducting the war. "To see this mission through," he noted, "Congress should encourage the President to use all necessary means to overcome and destroy this enemy, in what will be a long and trying campaign for freedom. Under the Constitution, the President already possesses this authority, but it is enhanced, and our cause strengthened, by the support of the Congress. . . . Let us give our Commander in Chief all necessary authority."[75] Given that the resolution received unanimous support in the Senate, McCain was like all senators who were ready to support aggressive military action. What is different, however, is that McCain not only provided policy support for the forthcoming war but also maintained that there was constitutional backing for a president with unlimited military powers. These views contrasted with those expressed by Senator Joe Biden, as discussed in chapter 1, who argued that Senate Joint Resolution 23 provided appropriate limitations on the commander in chief.[76] Similarly, Senators Carl Levin and John Kerry also maintained that suitable constitutional checks were in place against the president and that Congress had carried out its war powers duties.[77] Although a case can be made that such views exaggerated the de facto "limits" placed on the commander in chief, it is still clear that these positions were much different from McCain's, who argued that this vote was useful politically but unnecessary on constitutional grounds.

In 2002, Senate Joint Resolution 45, Authorization for the Use of Military Force against Iraq Resolution, received more deliberation than

Senate Joint Resolution 23, authorizing force against al-Qaeda, but again McCain was one senator who helped assure its passage. During these debates, he not only expressed political support for a strike on Iraq but also made extensive claims for presidential war powers by opposing any effort to limit or constrain the president.

In the debates over the possibility of military action against Iraq in 2002, Senator Robert Byrd proposed an amendment to place a time limit on the authorization for the use of force. The authorization would "terminate 12 months after the date of enactment of [the] joint resolution, except that the President may extend" the authorization under certain conditions.[78] In keeping with his long-held views on expansive presidential war powers authority, McCain opposed the resolution, noting that "to deprive the President 12 months from now of the authority we would grant him in this resolution would be an infringement on the authority of the Commander in Chief."[79]

In these same debates, Senator Byrd also attempted to require that the president be able to use force only under certain conditions. He maintained that only if there is "a clear threat of imminent, sudden, and direct attack upon the United States, its possessions or territories, or the Armed Forces of the United States" does the president have the authority to use armed force.[80] McCain opposed this amendment as well and instead made the case for preemptive military action. "Preventive action to target rogue regimes," he stated, "is not only imaginable but necessary. . . . The Byrd amendment would negate any congressional resolution authorizing the President to use all means to protect America from the threat posed by Iraq."[81]

In opposing Byrd's efforts, McCain further expounded: "This amendment regarding the preservation of Congress's constitutional authority is unnecessary. A portion of the amendment that would limit the authority of the President to wage war is arguably unconstitutional. The Congress can declare war, but it cannot dictate to the President how to wage war. No law passed by Congress could alter the constitutional separation of powers."[82] Additional insights on McCain's views were evident when Senator Carl Levin proposed an amendment that the president have the power to use force against Iraq only under a UN Security Council resolution that authorized all member nations to use force to eliminate the threat of certain weapons.[83] Levin's purpose was to keep the president from acting unilaterally. The amendment also stated that if a UN Security Council resolution were not adopted, the president would need to convene Congress to "consider proposals relative to Iraq."[84]

In response, McCain predictably argued against this effort. "Our country," he noted, "must [not] delegate our national security decision making to the United Nations. . . . This body should allow the executive branch the leeway to conduct diplomacy at the U.N.—not try to micromanage it from the Senate floor."[85] Thus, on Iraq, to a much greater extent than on Afghanistan, McCain pushed for the broadest possible war powers for the commander in chief. In doing so, he supported a resolution that permitted the president wide discretion in determining how and when military force would be used and removed Congress from its key constitutional duty in making that determination.[86]

Some senators do not achieve or seek national prominence and thus remain back benchers during their legislative careers. This is not the case for the two senators examined here. They have held senior leadership positions in their parties throughout their careers and have often sought to shape national debates, especially in the area of U.S. foreign policy. As was evident in chapter 4, Senators Kerry and McCain played leading roles in shaping the constitutional and legislative debate for the use of force in Libya in 2011—the largest military operation initiated during President Obama's first term. As was also established earlier, senior members of Congress can play decisive roles in shaping national policy and military decisions through either their legislative activism or their deferential behavior, which is why this chapter focused on two of the Senate's most frequent and arguably most significant voices in foreign policy in order to determine their roles in shaping war powers questions.

The findings demonstrate that Senators Kerry and McCain have worked to protect the commander in chief across the entirety of their congressional careers, with few exceptions. Both senators have on many occasions advanced the idea that it is the president alone who shall determine if and when U.S. military force will be used abroad. Senator McCain has employed a view of the Constitution that provides nearly unlimited authority for the commander in chief to make war decisions for the United States, and for the most part he has been generally nonpartisan in making these claims. Kerry argued at various times for the constitutional idea of checks and balances for entering war and for the WPR's necessity in the abstract, but in practice he supported nearly every presidential war during his entire Senate career. Whether it was Grenada in 1983, Panama in 1989, Haiti in 1994, or the Iraq War in 2003, both McCain and Kerry helped empower the commander in chief, and they did so again when President Obama used force in Libya in 2011. When members of Congress raised constitutional and WPR objections against Obama's actions, Kerry and McCain—as they had done in the past—worked to protect the president's asserted military powers. Thus, two senior and arguably national leaders in the U.S. Senate have helped frame the war power debates since the 1980s and continued to do so in the Obama administration's first term. Contrary to Founding Father Elbridge Gerry's arguments, they have worked repeatedly to place full military decision authority in the president's hands. Kerry's and McCain's legislative records provide some insight on why meaningful reform of the imbalance of power between the legislative and executive branches and ironically the sort of reform for "joint decision making for war" Senator Joe Biden advocated have made such little progress in the U.S. Congress.

7

Syria and Beyond

During his first term as president, Barack Obama demonstrated that as commander in chief, one executive office practice remained firmly entrenched. Like his predecessors since the Second World War, Obama maintained that a president may use military force without congressional approval. Whether it be with respect to two major troop surges in Afghanistan involving thousands of American forces or to hundreds of drone strikes in Pakistan, Yemen, and Somalia or to military and naval operations aimed at fighting pirates on the ocean and on land or to the firing of hundreds of missiles against Libya's military forces and leaders, he argued that those decisions belonged to *him,* not to Congress.

Much like previous Congresses since the Second World War, the two Congresses that faced President Obama in his first term likewise maintained its norm of deference to the commander in chief, sometimes actively working to avoid legislative responsibility for the use of force. The clearest case of this behavior occurred with the military strikes in Libya, when Speaker of the House John Boehner (R–Ohio) actively suppressed advocates of congressional war powers Representatives Dennis Kucinich (D–Ohio), Justin Amash (R–Mich.), and others who sought to compel Congress to take legislative responsibility for this use of force. In this case and in others, as Stephen Weissman has argued, understanding the roles of senior members of Congress is critical in uncovering the U.S. foreign-policy process, wherein Congress often defers to the commander in chief.[1] Similar deferential behavior was witnessed from congressional leaders regarding U.S. counterpiracy actions: Representatives Frank LoBiondo (R–N.J.) and Elijah Cummings (D–Md.) called for aggressive mili-

114 OBAMA AT WAR

tary action against pirates, yet they did not see the need for any explicit legislative approval for these uses of force, despite military actions that entailed the use of U.S. Special Forces and Navy SEALs and on occasion the rescue of foreign nationals on non-U.S. ships. Regarding the troop surges in Afghanistan, only a small group of liberal House Democrats raised substantive concern about and opposition to Obama's surge plans. On the uses of drones, leaders of the Senate and House Intelligence Committees similarly made the case that no further legislative oversight was needed and that the commander in chief could continue with his military policies. When Dennis Kucinich and Ron Paul (R–Tex.) called for more legislative oversight of Obama's uses of drones, congressional leaders chastised them, arguing that such oversight was inappropriate and unnecessary. When approving the LRA and Northern Uganda Recovery Act of 2009, Congress managed to grant the president expansive discretion for determining the best political, military, diplomatic, and economic strategy for capturing or killing Joseph Kony and other LRA leaders. Through such open-ended and ambiguous legislation and a legislative process that did not force members of Congress to record individual and countable votes for the legislation, members of Congress avoided legislative responsibility, which eventually resulted in the deployment of one hundred American Special Forces to Central Africa. Although Senator Russ Feingold (D–Wisc.) later argued that Congress had not approved of military action in this case, it is easy to see how this legislative process nevertheless further empowered the commander in chief.

Regarding the four major cases of military action taken in Obama's first term surveyed here, the findings also indicate that congressional leaders were actively nonpartisan in their practice of allowing the commander in chief to determine when and how force is used abroad. Though other research maintains that Congress and especially the party opposing the president often play a substantive role in checking the president and even "stops wars,"[2] the practices witnessed during Obama's first term strongly suggest otherwise. The legislative histories of senior senators such as John McCain (R–Ariz.) and John Kerry (D–Mass.) indicate long records of actively working and sometimes leading the effort in Congress to *empower* the commander in chief. Both worked to defend the practice of unilateral executive-branch military decisions and oftentimes did so for a president from the opposing party. Prior to Kerry's appointment as secretary of state in 2013, these two senators, who specialized in U.S. foreign and military policy during their service as members of the Senate Armed Services Committee (McCain) and the Senate Foreign Relations Committee (Kerry), played crucial roles in helping different commanders in chief use force without congressional authorization. This practice has continued through the Obama administration and is most clearly evident in the U.S. military strikes in Libya.

Syria, Congress, and War Powers

With the passing of his first term, Barack Obama again faced a crisis that galvanized much of the world's attention: the civil war in Syria. He had already sent what ostensibly was a clear signal to Syrian president Bashar al-Assad that the use of chemical weapons on the Syrian people was not acceptable and would constitute the crossing of a U.S. foreign-policy "red line."[3] The policy threat extended here seemed unmistakable; a chemical weapons strike would likely result in U.S. military action. This line was most egregiously crossed on August 21, 2013, when the Syrian government utilized chemical weapons, including sarin, mustard, and VX gases, across areas of Damascus where governmental opposition forces resided, resulting in the deaths of approximately 1,429 people, including 426 children. In releasing their evidence of the attack, the Obama administration also argued that the "Syrian regime" had carried out smaller chemical weapons attacks "multiple times in the last year."[4] NGOs, including Doctors Without Borders, provided similar accounts of a widespread chemical weapons attack.[5]

Within days of the massacre, the Obama administration began to mobilize for possible military action. It initially acted much as it had before, with implicit arguments for the president's independent authority to initiate military force. At the forefront of the push for a potential military response was Secretary of State John Kerry.[6] Though he did not clearly articulate the administration's constitutional rationale, by August 30, 2013, he made it clear that the Obama administration felt that military action would be a justifiable and appropriate response in this circumstance.[7] When specifically addressing the issue of military strikes, Kerry noted, "Now, we know that after a decade of conflict, the American people are tired of war. Believe me, I am, too. But fatigue does not absolve us of our responsibility." He added, "The President has been clear: Any action that *he might decide to take* will be a limited and tailored response to ensure that a despot's brutal and flagrant use of chemical weapons is held accountable." As he had done when in the Senate, he noted the ongoing value of consultation with Congress, implying that Congress has a power equal to the president's in making use-of-force decisions, but he also clearly stated that a use-of-force decision was for the president to make at his own discretion—once again contradicting himself, as he had done in the past.[8]

Secretary of Defense Chuck Hagel also clearly backed the president's independent military authority, which contrasts sharply with the views he expressed after he left the U.S. Senate and before his appointment as secretary of defense. In his 2008 book *America: Our Next Chapter,* Hagel wrote about Congress's institutional war powers failures regarding the 2003 Iraq war. "It is shocking," he noted, "how little Congress or the media challenged the Bush administration. Both political parties failed to do their job in Congress. Congress abdicated its oversight responsibilities and fell silent and timid."[9] Yet now as secretary of defense in 2013, following in line with the similar transformations of Senators Obama and Biden in their transition from the legislative branch to the executive branch, Hagel stated that the Defense Department had "moved assets in place to be able to fulfill and comply with whatever options the president wishes to take." He added that "we are ready to go."[10]

On the evening of August 30, 2013, with the momentum for military action increasing substantially, Obama surprised most of his key foreign-policy advisors upon returning from an evening walk with White House chief of staff Denis McDonough and indicated that he would like to seek explicit congressional approval before launching any military strikes.[11] The following day, in a public address the president noted, "I have decided that the United States should take military action against Syrian regime targets," yet added, "But having made my decision as Commander-in-Chief based on what I am convinced is our national security interests, I'm also mindful that I'm the President of the world's oldest constitutional democracy. I've long believed that our power is rooted not just in military might, but in our example as a government of the people, by the people, and for the people. And that's why I've made a second decision: I will seek authorization for the use of force from the American people's representatives in Congress." He continued, "Yet, while I believe I have the authority to carry out this military action without specific congressional authorization, I know that the country will be stronger if we take this course."[12]

Although no military conflict in recent American history is perfectly comparable to possible U.S. intervention in Syria's civil war, Obama's decision to turn to Congress in this case had some recent precedent. As noted in chapter 1, before the military action in Afghanistan in 2001, President George W. Bush turned to Congress for legislative approval to act. He similarly sought some form of congressional consent for waging war against Iraq in 2003, even though administration officials continued to assert that they had authority to use force without specific congressional authorization.[13] In the immediate days before U.S. and NATO air strikes in Kosovo in 1999, President Clinton also requested legislative approval to act, noting, "Without regard to our differing views on the Constitution about the use of force, I ask for your legislative support as we address the crisis in Kosovo."[14]

Nonetheless, as summarized in chapter 1 and noted by many other observers of American war powers practices, many examples exist of commanders in chief who did not request congressional approval to act. President Ronald Reagan carried out combat operations in Grenada in 1983 and launched air strikes on Libyan leader Muammar Qaddafi in 1986 without congressional approval or consultation. President George H. W. Bush deployed forces into combat missions in Panama in 1989 without seeking or requesting congressional approval. Bill Clinton did not gain congressional approval prior to the deployment of 10,000 troops to Haiti in 1994 or for his administration's bombings in Bosnia in 1995.[15] In this respect, Obama's sudden procedural change and turn to Congress surprised many in the political arena. At the same time, it is equally important to recognize that Obama, much like other commanders in chief, even when turning to Congress, still asserted what he felt was his independent military authority to use force.

Bipartisan Deference from Congress's Senior Leaders

At first glance, it may appear that Congress was quite assertive institutionally in challenging the president's ostensibly preferred course of military action against the Syria government. It is indisputable that many members of Congress actively challenged President Obama and the administration's argument for independent military action. Among those who led the opposition, Congressman Justin Amash opposed the president on constitutional grounds, as he had done when Obama used force in Libya, arguing that legislative approval was required before the president could take such action. Amash was especially active in expressing his opposition through social media, demanding that Speaker of the House John Boehner call the House back into session to address the issue.[16] On August 28, 2013, in some show of challenge to Obama's movement toward military action, Speaker Boehner himself also called upon Obama to increase his consultation with Congress and provided a list of questions for the president to answer regarding the policy implications of a military strike in Syria.[17]

The most concerted challenge to Obama's constitutional claims came from Congressman Scott Rigell (R–Va.), who by August 28, 2013—prior to Obama's turn to Congress on August 31—managed to gain the signatures of 116 members of Congress, including 18 Democrats, on a letter to the president expressing opposition to any unilateral decision to take military action in Syria. "We strongly urge you to consult and receive authorization from Congress before ordering the use of U.S. military force in Syria," the letter stated in its first paragraph. "Your responsibility to do so is prescribed in the Constitution and the War Powers Resolution of 1973."[18] The signatories represented more than one-fourth of all House members, and thus the letter was a significant challenge to the president's asserted authority to use force.

What is remarkable in the list of signatures, however, is the near complete bipartisan absence of Congress's senior party leaders as well as a dearth of Congress's foreign-policy leaders. Among the House Republican Party leadership, the only senior leader to sign the letter was Congressman James Lankford (R–Okla.), the Republican Policy Committee chair. Missing from the list were the signatures of Speaker of the House John Boehner, majority leader Eric Cantor (R–Va.), majority whip Kevin McCarthy (R–Calif.), and Republican Conference chair Cathy McMorris Rodgers (R–Wash.). Others who did not sign the letter include House Armed Services Committee chair Howard "Buck" McKeon (R–Tex.), House Armed Services Committee vice chair Mac Thornberry (R–Tex.), and House Intelligence Committee chair Mike Rogers (R–Mich.). Similarly, none of the Democratic Party leadership signed Rigell's letter, including minority leader Nancy Pelosi (D–Calif.), minority whip Steny Hoyer (D–Md.), assistant Democratic leader James Clyburn (D–S.C.), and Democratic Caucus chair Xavier Becerra (D–Calif.). The minority ranking members of the House Intelligence Committee and the Armed Services Committee also did not sign the letter.[19] Much like the responses to Obama's previous military actions, Congress's leaders—in nearly unanimous fashion—chose *not* to associate themselves with those members who most explicitly called for Congress to exercise its constitutional war powers. Among the leadership, a degree of bipartisan deference was once again the norm.

Some congressional leaders actively sided with President Obama regarding the use of force in the absence of congressional authorization. Perhaps without surprise, given his record, Senator John McCain, along with Senator Lindsey Graham (R–S.C.), criticized the president for not taking military action in the immediate aftermath of the chemical weapons strikes.[20] Eliot Engel (D–N.Y.), the ranking minority member of the House Foreign Affairs Committee, also expressed his support for presidential military action, noting, "I think we have to respond, and we have to act rather quickly. We can't afford to sit back and wait for the United Nations. . . . We can destroy the Syrian air force."[21]

Though House Armed Services Committee chair Buck McKeon's position evolved over time to become more opposed to U.S. military action, his initial response was, "Now that American credibility is on the line, the president cannot fail to act decisively," thus implicitly granting the commander in chief the authority to act.[22] A number of senators also expressed their backing for military strikes, including both parties' senior leaders of the Senate Foreign Relations Committee, Chairman Robert Menendez (D–N.J.) and ranking minority member Bob Corker (R–Tenn.).[23] Thus, although there indeed was meaningful opposition to Obama's planned course of military action prior to his August 31 turn to Congress, it was not publicly visible among Congress's senior leaders from either side of the aisle. Rather, they simply responded with either bipartisan deference or in some cases explicit statements of support for military strikes without legislative approval.

Once the president turned to Congress to request legislative support, more congressional opposition became evident. The *Washington Post,* among a number of other news outlets, argued that it appeared unlikely that Obama had enough support to win a resolution in favor of U.S. military action in Syria, with many members expressing opposition to military force and many others publicly remaining in the "undecided" category. Only a small minority explicitly backed the president.[24] Yet despite the opposition from rank-and-file members of Congress, most of Congress's senior leaders from both parties again rallied behind the president. Almost immediately after Obama requested congressional approval, the House's most senior Republican leadership, Speaker Boehner and majority leader Cantor, indicated that they would vote in favor of a resolution.[25] Similarly, House Democratic Party leaders Nancy Pelosi, Steny Hoyer, and Xavier Becerra indicated that they backed the president. Both Pelosi and Hoyer also added that although they were pleased Obama had reached out to Congress, they also felt he was not required by the Constitution to do so.[26] Ranking minority Democrat on the House Intelligence Committee, Dutch Ruppersberger (D–Md.), also signaled his support for strikes.[27] In one of the stranger positions taken, House Armed Services Committee chair Buck McKeon indicated that he might be able to support Obama if spending cuts were removed from the proposed defense budget; McKeon appeared ready to trade his vote for military action as long as Obama increased defense spending in general.[28]

It may be that these senior leaders were being passive-aggressive toward the president by simultaneously signaling their support for military strikes and doing little to help lobby and win votes for Obama's position. Nancy Pelosi indicated that she understood if members of Congress voted their "conscience" on this resolution, suggesting that at least among the Democratic caucus she would understand a "no" vote for the resolution.[29] Yet both party leaders also quickly rallied to support the president, ostensibly in an effort to rapidly signal their positions to rank-and-file members, which again entails a degree of deference to the commander in chief. Moreover, even if the senior leaders were utilizing a passive-aggressive strategy against the president, their position still suggests that they felt it was publicly unacceptable for senior party leaders to openly challenge a commander in chief as he moved toward military action. Instead, they apparently felt that they could express any legitimate opposition only in a subdued, tepid manner. Regardless of the motivation and strategy in play, what is clear is that nearly all senior party leaders were ready to support the commander in chief's desire to use force—both before he turned to Congress for its formal backing and then once again when he explicitly requested their support.

Given that this resolution was withdrawn from Congress once a diplomatic negotiation succeeded in initiating the removal of Syria's chemical weapons, we will never know if Congress would have refused an authorization to use force. That the crisis in Syria serves as an indicator of heightened congressional activism on war powers, however, seems unlikely. The political context in which Obama began to make his case for military action is important to understand. With his proposed use of force in Syria, Obama had very little international support. Even the United Kingdom, arguably America's closest ally, voted against an authorization to use force in this case.[30] In addition to British opposition, other NATO allies, including Germany and Poland, opposed military action, which indicated that if the Obama administration did proceed with military action, it would not have NATO's backing either.[31] At the UN, the United States was certainly not going to receive backing from the Security Council either, due in part to Russia's vehement opposition to military action. Moreover, in the United States by early September 2013 domestic public opinion was soundly against a military strike, with nearly 60 percent of Americans opposed.[32] Previous research on American public opinion and the use of force suggests that in such conditions—that is, when the United States uses force abroad without allied support and the situation does not involve clear and direct national-security interests—domestic opposition is likely to be high, which appeared evident in this case.[33] Even Pope Francis, the ostensible authority on the Catholic Church's Just War Doctrine, made a plea for peace rather than additional military strikes, which many interpreted as a direct challenge to possible U.S. military action.[34]

With all of these political challenges in place, coupled with an especially assertive faction of House Tea Party Republicans, President Obama faced widespread domestic and international opposition to a military strike. Presidents have in the past initiated military deployments even when faced with considerable domestic opposition; President Clinton did in Haiti in 1994 and Bosnia in 1995, and he had approval from the UN Security Council in both cases. In contrast, Obama had very little international support for military strikes in Syria. The likelihood that similar conditions will be repeated is difficult to predict, but it is challenging to find generally analogous examples of presidents initiating military action abroad when confronted with both strong domestic and international opposition.

Two constants in the war powers interplay were evident, however, in the controversy over Syria. First, although Obama requested congressional approval for military action, he also asserted and repeated what he believed was his perceived authority to use force without explicit legislative backing, just as his predecessors had. Second, Congress's leaders, almost in unanimous fashion, again acquiesced and deferred to the commander in chief—a theme that has been evident across all of Obama's military actions. This norm of executive dominance and legislative deference from Congress's senior leaders in war-making decisions for the United States raises the question of what can be done to restore a constitutional process for determining when the United States will use force.

Possible Solutions to the War Powers Imbalance

One route that has proven nearly futile in rectifying the executive–legislative war powers imbalance is a request for judicial intervention on Congress's behalf. In the modern era, the federal courts have expressed some sympathy for the argument that U.S. military action abroad requires explicit congressional authorization, but they have also avoided providing a remedy for the executive–legislative imbalance. The judiciary's aversion to intervening to rectify this imbalance is interesting given that the Supreme Court ruled on the constitutionality of war in its earliest years. In *Talbot v. Seeman* (5 U.S. 1) in 1801, the Court reiterated Congress's war powers authority for a variety of potential military operations: "the whole powers of war being by the Constitution of the United States vested in Congress."[35] In 1806 in the federal circuit case *United States v. Smith* (27 Fed. Cas. 1192, 1229 C.C.N.Y.), this Court also ruled that only Congress may authorize the use of force abroad. Presidents may repel sudden attacks, but it is Congress that shall determine when force may be used.[36] However, since the decision advanced in *United States v. Curtiss-Wright Export Corporation* (299 U.S. 304) in 1936, in which Justice George Sutherland misinterpreted a speech made by Congressman John Marshall in 1800 to argue that the president is the "sole organ of the federal government in the field of international relations,"[37] and especially in the aftermath of the Vietnam War, when the Supreme Court rejected constitutional war powers questions, the federal courts have shied away from war powers, either calling them not ripe for judicial intervention or arguing that political questions are best reserved for the political branches rather than the legal branch.[38] Thus, judicial efforts such as *Dellums v. Bush* (752 F. Supp. 1141 [D.C. Fed. Ct.]) in 1990, when President George H. W. Bush was moving toward war with Iraq without congressional approval, or *Campbell v. Clinton* (52 F.2d 34 [D.C. Cir.]) in 1999, led by Congressman Thomas Campbell (R–Calif.) when President Clinton used force in Kosovo without explicit legislative approval, failed to result in judicial remedies. Congressman Dennis Kucinich's effort in *Kucinich et al. v. Obama* (821 F. Supp. 2d 110), in which he and nine other members of Congress challenged the constitutionality of President Obama's military actions in Libya, faced a similar end when it too was dismissed from consideration.[39]

In addition to the federal courts' unreceptiveness to Congress's war powers appeals, few members of Congress choose to utilize the courts on war powers. As just noted, only 10 members of Congress appealed to the Federal District Court during the strikes on Libya even though 148 members of Congress sided with Kucinich in his House floor vote calling for a cessation of military action in fifteen days in early June 2011. The relatively small number of members who joined the suit suggests that most in Congress view a lawsuit as a futile attempt to produce change or simply do not want to be associated with a lawsuit against the president of the United States. Similarly, only 54 members of Congress in 1990 signed on to Congressman Ron Dellums's (D–Calif.) lawsuit against President Bush in response to the Bush administration's claims that it did not need Congress's approval to go to war with Iraq. To be clear, barely 10 percent of the entire Congress was willing to challenge judicially the constitutionality of Bush's sweeping claims of authority to wage war in Iraq in 1990 without congressional authorization. These small numbers also suggest a degree of deference in that some members of Congress may be willing to vote against a president on the rare occasions when such votes are taken, but most of them resist the next step of turning to the courts to request a judicial remedy.[40] Thus, members of Congress themselves have little faith in the courts on this issue, and given the federal courts' long history of avoiding these foreign-policy questions, a judicial solution to this constitutional imbalance of power seems unlikely.

As Joe Biden proposed while serving in the U.S. Senate, other legislative proposals have sought to address the president's perceived "imperial" behavior and Congress's repeated abdication to the commander in chief. The most recent legislative attempt centered around the ideas advanced by two former secretaries of state: James Baker and Warren Christopher. In their proposed War Powers Consultation Act of 2009, they first noted what nearly all the scholarship on war powers has found: that the WPR is a failure and that Congress has been removed from much of the decision-making processes regarding war. Their act then speaks about the need to restore a constitutional balance between the legislative and executive branches.[41]

When Baker and Christopher lobbied for their proposal, some members of Congress were interested in addressing this issue.[42] The proposal, however, was full of constitutionally suspect ideas as well as significant loopholes that, like the WPR itself, invited more ambiguity and debates on semantics, which then would help even further empower the president. The proposal permitted the president to use force without legislative approval for seven days in "significant armed conflict." In other words, presidents could conduct war for a week before legislative approval was required, which surely runs directly counter to the idea of Congress's constitutional role in declaring war. In addition, the proposed act also permitted the president to deploy and use force if necessary in humanitarian operations, rescue or training missions, and covert operations, all without specific legislative endorsement. These different kinds of operations invite new debates over what actually is a "humanitarian operation" or a simple "training mission." The criticism from legal experts was almost immediate, and beyond a couple of congressional committee hearings the proposal slipped quickly from Congress's agenda.[43] Although this interest in reform was commendable and the proposals for addressing the imbalance of power were well intentioned, these hearings and subsequent criticisms made clear the challenges in advancing new legislative remedies akin to an updated and improved WPR.

Some hope for renewed assertions of Congress's war powers came in the 2010 midterm elections when a number of Tea Party–affiliated Republicans won seats in the Senate and House of Representatives. Although the group lacked a central leader and purposely avoided a clear statement of principles, it was generally evident that it favored a stricter interpretation and application of the Constitution.[44] Tea Party activists, as noted earlier, have a history of advocating for Congress's war powers.[45] Thus, when President Obama commenced military operations in Libya without congressional authorization, as addressed in chapter 4, a number of Tea Party–affiliated members, including Congressman Justin Amash, rose to challenge Obama's constitutional claims. In the Senate, Rand Paul (R–Ky.) and a handful of other Tea Party senators also challenged the president. Nonetheless, these efforts did not manage to generate followers, and perhaps due to the challengers' legislative inexperience and to senior leaders' efforts to make sure that Congress would not have to vote explicitly either for or against the operation, the Tea Party momentum on war powers was handily defeated.

Generating greater congressional activity on war powers will likely require the attention of Congress's senior leadership to challenge prevailing practice and demand a more substantive decision-making role for Congress on war. Indeed, members of Congress in recent times have demonstrated leadership across a host of national-security issues, and some of them, due to the force of their personal interest as well as to their more senior stature, have been able to shape major national-security questions by challenging presidents. Senator Sam Nunn (D–Ga.), in office from 1972 to 1997, is often credited with placing considerable pressure on NATO allies and leaders to encourage higher defense spending in Europe, well beyond what the Reagan administration was publicly advocating.[46] Senator Richard Lugar (R–Ind.) shaped U.S. foreign policy in the 1980s by aggressively pushing for condemnation of South Africa and its apartheid policies. Lugar also called for greater protection of human rights and for recognizing Corazon Aquino as the legitimate winner of the 1986 presidential elections in the Philippines when incumbent president Ferdinand Marcos claimed victory in what many viewed as a stolen election.[47] Political scientist Brien Hallett also calls attention to Senator Malcomb Wallop (R–Wy.), who in a deliberative and well-reasoned manner made the case for a strong and healthy constitutional debate over President George H. W. Bush's actions prior to the war in Iraq in 1991. In Hallett's view, Wallop represents precisely what the Congress needs for a thoughtful debate on the merits and political utility of declaring war.[48] In 1993, Senator Robert Byrd (D–W.V.) also threatened the Clinton administration with an invocation of the WPR upon the death of eighteen U.S.

Army Rangers. The extent of Byrd's influence is not clear, but in the after-math of this tragedy, coupled with a shift in public opinion and Byrd's pressure on the president, Clinton quickly adopted a new military strategy for dealing with the problems in Somalia.[49] Previous chapters have high-lighted occasional flashes of courage from other members of Congress who were not afraid to challenge the prevailing norm advanced by senior leaders and instead invoked calls for Congress to exercise its constitutional duties to check the president prior to warfare. When President Obama authorized bombings in Libya, highlighted in chapter 4, Congressman Dennis Kucinich—as he had done previously in response to a number of military operations—pressed his fellow members of Congress to assert their constitutional war powers.[50] These examples highlight the possibil-ity that members of Congress have the potential to change the president's national-security and foreign-policy decision-making process, including the prospect for influencing America's entry into war. Members of Con-gress have risked condemnation by their party leaders and in some cases by their own party's president when challenging the deferential norm in Congress and the commander in chief's own asserted war powers.

Nonetheless, as the cases in this book demonstrate, it is still difficult for a member of Congress to defeat senior party leaders who are deter-mined to place all political and constitutional responsibility for U.S. military action in the president's hands. Apart from Congressman John Murtha's (D–Pa.) public challenge to President Bush during the Iraq War, which caused considerable alarm within the White House and Pen-tagon,[51] it is difficult to find examples of senior Democrats who exercised similar degrees of influence on U.S. foreign policy during the most recent Bush administration, as Senators Nunn and Byrd had earlier challenged Reagan and Clinton, respectively. Thomas E. Ricks argues that few Dem-ocrats, especially Democratic presidential contenders in the George W. Bush era, wanted to be viewed on the "wrong side" of the Iraq issue and thus allowed the Bush war plan to proceed with limited challenge. When Senator Byrd rose to challenge Bush and assert Congress's war powers, even after senior Democratic leaders advised him "to get out of the way as soon as possible," he made an impassioned case for not rushing into war. Nonetheless, Byrd, who could readily quote Greek philosophers and bibli-cal passages, was well past his political prime by that time and "had little influence even in his own party."[52] Despite the facts that Operation Iraqi

Freedom was initiated under two faulty premises—that Saddam Hussein had weapons of mass destruction and had connections to al-Qaeda—and that the United States was experiencing more casualties in Iraq than in any war since Vietnam, Congress's senior Democratic leadership was still generally unwilling to wage sustained challenges to President Bush and his war authority, so it is difficult to be optimistic about the future prospects of Congress's assertion of its constitutional war powers. As in the Bush era, in the Obama era Congress's senior leaders in both parties have willingly followed along with the president's war plans and ambitions. Thus, unless President Obama or his successors request explicit congressional approval for a military operation that has nearly no international support and few domestic backers, the current practice of executive leadership and *active* legislative deference is likely to continue.

More "Noise in the Process"

Despite what appear to be deeply embedded norms in the war powers interplay, it is worth recalling what America's Founding Fathers believed: that checks and balances are crucial and essential in a healthy democratic polity, especially when it comes to determining if that polity will enter war. Such decisions were meant to be made by the legislative branch because the Founding Fathers did not want them placed in the hands of one leader.[53] This basic principle of constitutional government cannot be discarded simply because a president thinks otherwise or because it is politically expedient to grant the commander in chief unilateral war powers. Such an approach runs directly counter to what the Founders advocated and what was practiced for much of U.S. history.[54]

It is also worth noting that a consolidation of war-making power in the executive poses significant foreign-policy risks to the United States. As witnessed in the planning process in the lead-up to the Iraq War, multiple mistakes were made, most notably in the kind of information provided to the president, the pronounced biases the president brought with him into the White House, the manner in which the president received information, and how the president himself organized key advisory roles.[55] Moreover, it has also been well established that American generals can make significant mistakes in their own war-planning processes and advisory roles to the president. American generals, including those in the Bush administration, have suffered from an inability to think strategically about the purpose and objectives in warfare.[56] Given these challenges in good decision making, all of which exist in the executive branch, it makes good strategic sense to push for more joint deliberation between the executive and legislative branches, for substantially stronger congressional oversight of the commander in chief, and for a Congress that accepts its constitutional war powers responsibilities. In 2008, former senator Chuck Hagel made the case well—somewhat ironically given his later stance as secretary of defense—when he called for meaningful congressional involvement in the decision to go to war: "When the people's representatives fail to weigh in on the fateful decision to go to war, both the people and the system that represents them are grievously harmed."[57]

Members of Congress must accept that their primary role is as *legislators* rather than as a cadre of full-time campaigners and fund-raisers, as has increasingly become evident. Many have relocated their staffs from Washington, D.C., to their congressional home districts, ostensibly in an effort to carry out greater constituency service workloads but most likely to generate higher numbers of patron–service relationships. Thomas Mann and Norman Ornstein provide compelling evidence that members of Congress conduct fewer committee hearings, have more truncated and rule-oriented floor debates, and spend less and less time in Washington, D.C.[58] Yet the congressional debate that ensued in 2011 over the constitutionality of President Obama's military action in Libya and the considerable opposition evident from rank-and-file members of Congress to military action in Syria in 2013 provide some reason for hope that a change is possible. Congress can and must "make noise about the process," as the Founding Fathers thought best. Such noise can help commanders in chief avoid mistakes that have profound strategic consequences for the United States and its allies and, in the best of all scenarios, help steer and shape national-security decisions that advance American principles and interests in the best way possible.

Acknowledgments

For a number of reasons, one of my favorite book titles is *No Man Is an Island,* by Trappist monk Thomas Merton, published in 1955 and who found another use for seventeenth-century poet John Donne's famous phrase. In my case, this phrase applies quite well because this book would have never happened without many others' help.

Normally, authors save the best for last. I will start with the best first. My wife, Tece, is my best friend, my guardian angel, and the love of my life. I thank her for supporting me in all my pursuits and interests.

Eastern Illinois University has been an excellent home in which to teach and carry out my research interests. Among my Eastern Illinois colleagues, I thank especially Jeff Ashley, Dave Carwell, Melinda Mueller, Rich Wandling, Bob Augustine, and Mary Anne Hanner. For excellent research assistance, I thank Michael Neureiter, Scott Trail, James Arthur, and Keneshbek Abdirakhmanov.

The reviewers of this manuscript provided excellent comments and constructive criticism. I am especially grateful to Lou Fisher, who has inspired my research for many years and who provided many useful recommendations for the manuscript.

Many of the chapters here appeared previously in different versions. Portions of chapter 1 and 2 were published as "War Powers in the Obama Administration," *Contemporary Security Policy* 31, no. 2 (2010): 204–24. Much of the research from chapters 3 and 4 appeared in "Somali Pirates, the American Military, and the U.S. Constitution: Congressional Oversight without Responsibility," *Illinois Political Science Review* 14 (2012): 53–71, and "Libya and American War Powers: War-Making Decisions in the United States," *Global Change, Peace, and Security* 25, no. 2 (2013): 175–89. A version of chapter 5 appeared as "Congress's Efforts to Defeat Joseph Kony and the Lord's Resistance Army: NGO Activism, Terrorism, and Evangelism," *Whitehead Journal of Diplomacy and International*

Relations 14, no. 1 (2013): 111–24. I did the research on Senator McCain initially with several colleagues, Jeremy L. Bowling, Richard D. Caldwell, and John S. Morris, and it appeared in our article "Congressional War Powers, the Commander in Chief, and Senator John McCain," *Southern California Interdisciplinary Law Journal* 18, no. 1 (2008): 1–16. I remain grateful to these colleagues. The research on Kerry in chapter 6 was previously published as "John Kerry as Commander in Chief: War Powers in the Kerry Administration," *Journal of Military and Strategic Studies* 7, no. 1 (2004): 1–22. I thank all previous manuscript reviewers and editors of the journals just noted, who helped me improve the research and avoid mistakes. Each article has been revised significantly for this book, and any errors remain mine alone.

I benefited also from presenting individual chapters to different professional organizations and academic institutions, where I often received useful comments and critiques, especially at St. Antony's College at Oxford, the International Studies Association, the Air War College, Eastern Kentucky University, Illinois State University, the Les Aspen Center for Government at Marquette University, and the Summer Workshop in International Security sponsored by the Arms Control, Disarmament, and International Security Program at the University of Illinois.

Many other people contributed to this book in different ways by commenting on individual chapters or simply by providing general support or advice for the project, including Don Wolfensberger, Fred Gagnon, Joe Hinchliffe, Pat James, John F. Schmitt, Mark Jerva, Thushara Dibley, and Kathy Anderson-Conner. I also thank Steve Wrinn for his interest in the manuscript and for his encouragement along the way.

Finally, the rest of the Hendricksons deserve lots of credit: Jerry, Mary, Daniel, Scott, Marguerite, Frances, and Ryan.

Notes

Introduction

1. Barack Obama, "Remarks to the White House Press Corps," August 20, 2012, at http://www.whitehouse.gov/the-press-office/2012/08/20/remarks-president-white-house-press-corps.

2. Quoted in John J. Kruzel, "Gates Discusses New Nuclear Posture, U.S. Relations with Karzi," American Forces Press Service, April 11, 2010, at http://www.defense.gov/news/newsarticle.aspx?id=58700.

3. Quoted in Chelsea J. Carter, "Obama: Iran More Than a Year Away from Developing Nuclear Weapon," CNN, March 15, 2013, at http://www.cnn.com/2013/03/14/world/meast/israel-obama-iran.

4. As noted in James Madison, *Notes of Debates in the Federal Convention of 1787 Reported by James Madison* (1966; reprint, New York: Norton, 1987), 476.

5. See Louis Fisher, *Presidential War Power,* 3rd ed. (Lawrence: University Press of Kansas, 2013).

6. Brien Hallett, *Declaring War: Congress, the President, and What the Constitution Does Not Say* (New York: Cambridge University Press, 2012), 2.

7. Barack Obama, "Transcript: 'This Is Your Victory' Says Obama," CNN, November 4, 2008, at http://edition.cnn.com/2008/POLITICS/11/04/obama.transcript/.

8. David E. Sanger, *Confront and Conceal: Obama's Secret Wars and Surprising Use of American Power* (New York: Crown, 2012).

9. Brad Plumer, "America's Staggering Defense Budget, in Charts," *Washington Post,* January 7, 2013, at http://www.washingtonpost.com/blogs/wonkblog/wp/2013/01/07/everything-chuck-hagel-needs-to-know-about-the-defense-budget-in-charts/. See also Center for Arms Control and Arms Proliferation, "U.S. Defense Spending vs. Global Defense Spending," April 24, 2013, at http://armscontrolcenter.org/issues/securityspending/articles/2012_topline_global_defense_spending/.

10. See Stephen R. Weissman, *A Culture of Deference: Congress's Failure of Leadership in Foreign Policy* (New York: Basic Books, 1995).

11. Cong. Rec. H2120 (March 31, 2011).

12. Senator Biden frequently uses the term *monarchism* in Joseph R. Biden Jr. and John B. Ritch III, "The War Power at a Constitutional Impasse: A 'Joint Decision' Solution," *Georgetown Law Journal* 77, no. 1 (1988): 381, and it is discussed at length in chapter 1.

13. Caroline D. Krass, "Authority to Use Force in Libya," Office of Legal

Counsel to the Attorney General, April 1, 2011, at http://www.lawfareblog.com /wp-content/uploads/2013/10/Memorandum-Opinion-from-Caroline-D.-Krass-Principal-Deputy-Assistant-Attorney-General-Office-of-Legal-Counsel-to-the-Attorney-General-Authority-to-Use-Military-Force-in-Libya-Apr.-1-2011.pdf.

14. Weissman, *A Culture of Deference;* Gerald Warburg, "Congress: Checking Presidential Power," in *The National Security Enterprise: Navigating the Labyrinth,* ed. Roger Z. George and Harvey Rishikof (Washington, D.C.: Georgetown University Press, 2011), 227–46.

15. Quoted in David Nakamura and Aaron Blake, "Obama on Ukraine: 'There Will Be Consequences If People Step over the Line,'" *Washington Post,* February 19, 2014, at http://www.washingtonpost.com/blogs/post-politics/wp/2014/02/19 /obama-on-ukraine-there-will-be-consequences-if-people-step-over-the-line/.

1. The War Powers Framework for the Obama Presidency

1. This issue is covered in chapter 4, although see, for example, Louis Fisher, "Military Operations in Libya: No War? No Hostilities?" *Presidential Studies Quarterly* 42, no. 1 (2012): 184–85; Michael J. Glennon, "The Cost of 'Empty Words': A Comment on the Justice Department's Libya Opinion," online feature, *Harvard National Security Journal,* April 14, 2011, at http://harvardnsj.org/2011/04 /the-cost-of-empty-words-a-comment-on-the-justice-departments-libya-opinion/.

2. White House, Office of the Press Secretary, "Press Conference by the President," June 29, 2011, at http://www.whitehouse.gov/the-press-office/2011/06/29 /press-conference-president.

3. James Madison, *Notes of Debates in the Federal Convention of 1787 Reported by James Madison* (1966; reprint, New York: Norton, 1987), 476. See also Michael D. Ramsey, "Textualism and War Powers," *University of Chicago Law Review* 69, no. 4 (2002): 1543–1638.

4. David Gray Adler, "The Constitution and Presidential Warmaking: The Enduring Debate," *Political Science Quarterly* 103, no. 1 (1988): 1–36; Charles A. Lofgren, "War-Making under the Constitution: The Original Understanding," *Yale Law Journal* 81, no. 4 (1972): 672–702. In contrast, see John Yoo, *The Powers of War and Peace: The Constitution and Foreign Affairs after 9/11* (Chicago: University of Chicago Press, 2005); John Tower, "Congress versus the President: The Formulation and Implementation of American Foreign Policy," *Foreign Affairs* 60, no. 2 (1981): 229–46.

5. Francis D. Wormuth and Edwin B. Firmage, *To Chain the Dog of War: The War Power of Congress in History and Law,* 2nd ed. (Urbana: University of Illinois Press, 1989).

6. Kenneth B. Moss, *Undeclared War and the Future of U.S. Foreign Policy* (Baltimore: Johns Hopkins University Press, 2008); Louis Fisher, *Presidential War Powers,* 3rd ed. (Lawrence: University of Press of Kansas, 2013); Gordon Silverstein, *Imbalance of Powers: Constitutional Interpretation and the Making of American*

Foreign Policy (New York: Oxford University Press, 1997); John Hart Ely, *War and Responsibility: Constitutional Lessons of Vietnam and Its Aftermath* (Princeton, N.J.: Princeton University Press, 1990); Michael J. Glennon, *Constitutional Diplomacy* (Princeton, N.J.: Princeton University Press, 1990); Harold Hongju Koh, *National Security Constitution: Sharing Power after the Iran–Contra Affair* (New Haven, Conn.: Yale University Press, 1990). For a wider discussion of congressional deference in foreign policy, see Stephen R. Weissman, *A Culture of Deference: Congress's Failure of Leadership in Foreign Policy* (New York: Basic Books, 1995).

7. Fisher, *Presidential War Power;* Michael J. Glennon, "The Constitution and Chapter VII of the United Nations Charter," *American Journal of International Law* 85, no. 1 (1991): 74–88; Matthew D. Berger, "Implementing a United Nations Security Council Resolution: The President's Power to Use Force with the Authorization of Congress," *Hastings International and Comparative Law Review* 15, no. 1 (1991): 83–109. For an alternative view, see David Golove, "From Versailles to San Francisco: The Revolutionary Transformation of the War Powers," *University of Colorado Law Review* 70, no. 4 (1999): 1491–1523.

8. Lawrence S. Kaplan, *The United States and NATO: The Formative Years* (Lexington: University Press of Kentucky, 1984): 115; Michael J. Glennon, "United States Mutual Security Treaties: The Commitment Myth," *Columbia Journal of Transnational Law* 24, no. 3 (1986): 530–32.

9. For recent scholarship on this issue, see Stephen M. Griffin, *Long Wars and the Constitution* (Cambridge, Mass.: Harvard University Press, 2013); Mariah Zeisberg, *War Powers: The Politics of Constitutional Authority* (Princeton, N.J.: Princeton University Press, 2013). See also Fisher, *Presidential War Power,* and Ryan C. Hendrickson, *The Clinton Wars: The Constitution, Congress, and War Powers* (Nashville: Vanderbilt University Press, 2002), 10.

10. War Powers Resolution, 50 U.S. Code, chap. 33, at http://www.law.cornell.edu/uscode/text/50/chapter-33.

11. President Carter expressed some rhetorical support for the WPR, as did the Clinton administration early in its tenure. See Hendrickson, *The Clinton Wars,* 13–19, 31–32.

12. Among the array of critics of the WPR, see Brien Hallett, *Declaring War: Congress, the President, and What the Constitution Does Not Say* (New York: Cambridge University Press, 2012); Timothy S. Boylan and Glenn A. Phelps, "The War Powers Resolution: A Rationale for Congressional Inaction," *Parameters* 31, no. 2 (2001): 109; Louis Fisher and David Gray Adler, "The War Powers Resolution: Time to Say Goodbye," *Political Science Quarterly* 113, no. 1 (1998): 1–20; Michael J. Glennon, "Too Far Apart: The War Powers Resolution," *University of Miami Law Review* 50, no. 1 (1995): 17–31; Edward Keynes, "The War Powers Resolution: A Bad Idea Whose Time Has Come and Gone," *University of Toledo Law Review* 23, no. 2 (1992): 343–62; Robert A. Katzmann, "War Powers: Toward a New Accommodation," in *A Question of Balance: The President, the Congress, and Foreign Policy,* ed. Thomas E. Mann (Washington, D.C.: Brookings Institution Press, 1990),

35–69; John Hart Ely, "Suppose Congress Wanted a War Powers Act That Worked," *Columbia Law Review* 88, no. 7 (1988): 1379–1431; Mark L. Krotoski, "Essential Elements of Reform of the War Powers Resolution," *Santa Clara Law Review* 29, no. 3 (1989): 607–752.

13. Hendrickson, *The Clinton Wars.* On Clinton's difficult relationship with the U.S. military, see Richard Kohn, "The Erosion of Civilian Control of the Military in the United States Today," *Naval War College Review* 55, no. 3 (2002): 9–59.

14. Ryan C. Hendrickson and Frédérick Gagnon, "The United States vs. Terrorism: Clinton, Bush, and Osama Bin Laden," in *Contemporary Cases in U.S. Foreign Policy,* 3rd ed., ed. Ralph G. Carter (Washington, D.C.: Congressional Quarterly Press, 2007), 1–24; Karl K. Schonberg, "Global Security and Legal Restraint: Reconsidering War Powers after September 11," *Political Science Quarterly* 119, no. 1 (2004): 115–42; Nancy Kassop, "The War Power and Its Limits," *Presidential Studies Quarterly* 33, no. 3 (2003): 509–29; David Abramowitz, "The President, the Congress, and Use of Force: Legal and Political Considerations in Authorizing Use of Force against International Terrorism," *Harvard International Law Journal* 43, no. 1 (2002): 73.

15. Mike Allen and Juliet Eilperin, "Bush Aides Say Iraq War Needs No Hill Vote," *Washington Post,* August 26, 2002.

16. Gary R. Hess, "Presidents and the Congressional War Resolutions in 1991 and 2002," *Political Science Quarterly* 121, no. 1 (2006): 93–118; Louis Fisher, "Deciding on War against Iraq: Institutional Failures," *Political Science Quarterly* 118, no. 3 (2003): 389–410.

17. George W. Bush, "Letter to Congressional Leaders on Further Deployment of United States Military Forces in Haiti," *Public Papers of the Presidents of the United States,* March 2, 2004, 295–96, at http://www.gpo.gov/fdsys/pkg/PPP-2004-book1/pdf/PPP-2004-book1-doc-pg295.pdf; Erika N. Cornelius and Ryan C. Hendrickson, "George W. Bush, War Powers, and U.N. Peacekeeping in Haiti," *White House Studies* 8, no. 1 (2008): 57–70. On Clinton in 1994, see Hendrickson, *The Clinton Wars,* chap. 3.

18. Sheryl Gay Stolberg, "A Symbolic Vote Is a Sign of Bitter Debates to Come," *New York Times,* February 17, 2007.

19. Thomas E. Ricks, *The Gamble: General David Petraeus and the American Military Adventure in Iraq, 2006–2008* (New York: Penguin, 2009), 150; Andrew J. Bacevich, *The Limits of Power: The End of American Exceptionalism* (New York: Holt, 2008), 69–71. On freshman Democrats' fears regarding aggressively challenging Bush on Iraq in 2007, see David Nather, "Mission: Win Back an Angry Base," *Congressional Quarterly Weekly,* May 28, 2007, 1570. See also Kelly McHugh, "Understanding Congress's Role in Terminating Unpopular Wars: A Comparison of the Vietnam and Iraq Wars," *Democracy and Security* 10, no. 3 (2014): 191–224.

20. For exceptions to the research on congressional deference, see William G. Howell and Jon C. Pevehouse, *While Dangers Gather: Congressional Checks on Presidential War Powers* (Princeton, N.J.: Princeton University Press, 2007) and "When

Congress Stops Wars," *Foreign Affairs* 86, no. 5 (2007): 95–107. On congressional assertiveness in foreign policy more broadly, see Ralph G. Carter and James M. Scott, *Choosing to Lead: Understanding Congressional Foreign Policy Entrepreneurs* (Durham, N.C.: Duke University Press, 2009), and Marie Henehan, *Foreign Policy and Congress: An International Relations Perspective* (Ann Arbor: University of Michigan Press, 2000).

21. Jack Goldsmith, *Power and Constraint: The Accountable Presidency after 9/11* (New York: Norton, 2012); David Gray Adler, "The Law: George Bush as Commander in Chief: Toward the Nether World of Constitutionalism," *Presidential Studies Quarterly* 36, no. 3 (2006): 525–40.

22. Congressman Abraham Lincoln (R–Ill.) entered the White House in 1861 with a previous record of quite aggressively challenging the president's war authority as commander in chief. See Louis Fisher, "The Mexican War and Lincoln's 'Spot Resolutions,'" *Law Library of Congress*, August 19, 2009, at http://www.loufisher .org/docs/wi/433.pdf, and Wormuth and Firmage, *To Chain the Dog of War*, 58. Otherwise, Biden and Obama are unique in their clear records of challenging presidential war authority prior to their positions in the executive branch.

23. Barton Gellman, *Angler: The Cheney Vice Presidency* (New York: Penguin, 2008); Joel K. Goldstein, "The Rising Power of the Modern Vice Presidency," *Presidential Studies Quarterly* 38, no. 3 (2008): 374–89; Bruce P. Montgomery, "Congressional Oversight: Vice President Richard B. Cheney's Executive Branch Triumph," *Political Science Quarterly* 120, no. 4 (2005–2006): 581–617.

24. Mark Leibovich, "Speaking Freely, Sometimes, Biden Finds Influential Role," *New York Times*, March 29, 2009.

25. Joseph R. Biden Jr. and John B. Ritch III, "The War Power at a Constitutional Impasse: A 'Joint Decision' Solution," *Georgetown Law Journal* 77, no. 1 (1988): 369–70.

26. Ibid., 374.

27. Quoted in ibid., 377–78.

28. Cong. Rec. S9444 (July 30, 1998).

29. Cong. Rec. 32619 (October 21, 1988).

30. Cong. Rec. S17706–24 (October 8, 1992).

31. Cong. Rec. S121 (January 10, 1991).

32. Cong. Rec. S3975 (March 15, 1995); Cong. Rec. S9444 (July 30, 1998).

33. Cong. Rec. S9444 (July 30, 1998).

34. Cong. Rec. 1339 (January 18, 1973).

35. Cong. Rec. 32354 (December 18, 1982).

36. Cong. Rec. 24046 (September 14, 1983).

37. Cong. Rec. 7683 (April 4, 1984).

38. Cong. Rec. 29850 (October 28, 1983).

39. Michael Rubner, "The Reagan Administration, the 1973 War Powers Resolution, and the Invasion of Grenada," *Political Science Quarterly* 100, no. 4 (1985–1986): 627–47.

40. Steve Gerstel, "Senate Challenged to Give Bush Authority to Use Military in Panama," United Press International, October 4, 1989.

41. Cong. Rec. S14333 (October 1, 1990).

42. Cong. Rec. S121 (January 10, 1991).

43. Ibid.

44. Cong. Rec. S17706 (October 8, 1992).

45. For example, on Bosnia, see Cong. Rec. S18497–99 (December 13, 1995); on Kosovo, see Cong. Rec. S4552 (March 3, 1999).

46. Cong. Rec. S16857 (November 20, 1993); S7966 (June 29, 1994); S3971 (March 15, 1995). See also Cong. Rec. S9444 (July 30, 1998).

47. Cong. Rec. S3118 (March 23, 1999).

48. Ivo Daalder, *Getting to Dayton: The Making of America's Bosnia Policy* (Washington, D.C.: Brookings Institution Press, 2000), 14.

49. Cong. Rec. S9423 (September 14, 2001).

50. Cong. Rec. S10235–37 (October 10, 2002). Regarding Biden's opposition to a preemptive military doctrine, see Cong. Rec. S10185 (October 9, 2002).

51. Cong. Rec. S10260 (October 10, 2002).

52. Fisher, "Deciding on War against Iraq."

53. Interview on *Hardball with Chris Matthews*, NBC, December 4, 2007, transcript at http://www.nbcnews.com/id/22114621/.

54. Katzmann, "War Powers."

55. Hendrickson, *The Clinton Wars*, 159.

56. Jeff Zeleny, "As Candidate, Obama Carves Antiwar Stance," *New York Times*, February 26, 2007.

57. Quoted in States News Service, "A Way Forward in Iraq," November 20, 2006, LexisNexis.

58. States News Service, "Obama Statement on Iraq," January 17, 2007, LexisNexis.

59. Cong. Rec. S722–23 (January 18, 2007).

60. Cong. Rec. S1343 (January 30, 2007).

61. Quoted in Nedra Pickler, "Obama Favors Removing U.S. Combat Forces by March 2008," Associated Press, January 31, 2007.

62. Charlie Savage, "Barack Obama's Q&A," *Boston Globe*, December 20, 2007, at http://www.boston.com/news/politics/2008/specials/CandidateQA/ObamaQA/.

63. Ibid.

64. Quoted in Peter Baker, "Obama to Hear Panel on Changes to War Powers Act," *New York Times on the Web*, December 12, 2008, at http://www.nytimes.com/2008/12/12/us/politics/11web-baker.html?_r=0.

65. Although Baker and Christopher's intent seems to have been centered on limiting presidential uses of force and encouraging greater congressional assertion of its war powers, critics of their proposal noted that the impact would likely be otherwise.

2. Afghanistan, Drone Warfare, and the Kill List

1. David Sanger, *Confront and Conceal: Obama's Secret Wars and Surprising Use of American Power* (New York: Crown), 243–72.

2. Stephen R. Weissman, *A Culture of Deference: Congress's Failure of Leadership in Foreign Policy* (New York: Basic Books, 1995).

3. Barack Obama, "Statement of United States Troop Levels in Afghanistan," *Daily Compilation of Presidential Documents,* February 17, 2009.

4. Barack Obama, "Remarks on United States Military and Diplomatic Strategies for Afghanistan and Pakistan," *Daily Compilation of Presidential Documents,* March 27, 2009.

5. Peter Baker and David M. Herszenhorn, "Obama Planning to Retain Military Tribunal System for Detainees," *New York Times,* May 15, 2009.

6. Gail Russell Chaddock, "Antiwar Activists Split over Obama's Afghanistan Policy," *Christian Science Monitor,* April 4, 2009, at http://www.csmonitor.com/2009/0404/p99s07-usgn.html.

7. Barack Obama, "Letter to Congressional Leaders on the Global Deployments of United States Combat-Equipped Armed Forces," *Public Papers of the Presidents of the United States,* June 15, 2009, 833–35.

8. Authorization for Use of Military Force, S.J. Res. 23, 107th Cong., 1st sess., September 18, 2001.

9. See, for example, Paul Gallis and Vincent Morelli, *NATO in Afghanistan: A Test of the Transatlantic Alliance* (Washington, D.C.: Congressional Research Service, July 18, 2008); Astri Suhrke, "A Contradictory Mission? Stabilization to Combat in Afghanistan," *International Peacekeeping* 15, no. 2 (2008): 214–36; Richard E. Rupp, *NATO after 9/11: An Alliance in Continuing Decline* (New York: Palgrave, 2006).

10. Edward Luce, "Afghanistan Throws Up Tough Choices for Obama," *Financial Times,* August 10, 2009.

11. Some of the actual new troop contributions in 2010 from Europe were difficult to calculate. See Craig Whitlock, "NATO Struggling to Fulfill Commitments for More Troops in Afghanistan," *Washington Post,* January 27, 2010.

12. Peter Baker, "How Obama Came to Plan for 'Surge' in Afghanistan," *New York Times on the Web,* December 6, 2009, at http://www.nytimes.com/2009/12/06/world/asia/06reconstruct.html?pagewanted=all.

13. For additional journalistic summaries of Congress's absence in this process, see Anne E. Kornblut, Scott Wilson, and Karen DeYoung, "Obama Pressed for Faster Surge," *Washington Post,* December 6, 2009. On Senator Kerry's role, see Peter Baker and Sabrina Tavernise, "U.S. Signals Delay in Afghan Troop Decision," *New York Times,* October 19, 2009.

14. Carl Hulse, "House Rejects Plan to Leave Afghanistan by Year's End," *New York Times on the Web,* March 10, 2010, at http://www.nytimes.com/2010/03/11/world/asia/11cong.html.

15. Emily Cadei and Frank Oliveri, "Capitol Hill's Own Afghanistan War,"

Congressional Quarterly Weekly, January 10, 2011; on the absence of national debate on Afghanistan, see David E. Sanger and Thom Shanker, "Two Campaigns Skirt Talk of Tough Choices in Afghanistan," *New York Times,* October 21, 2012, at http://www.nytimes.com/2012/10/22/us/politics/candidates-skirt-talk-of-hard-afghanistan-choices.html?pagewanted=all.

16. Sanger, *Confront and Conceal,* 256.

17. For a sample of the legal questions raised with Koh's defense, see http://insidejustice.com/law/index.php/intl/2010/03/26/asil_koh_drone_war_law.

18. Charlie Savage, "Secret U.S. Memo Made Legal Case to Kill a Citizen," *New York Times,* October 8, 2011.

19. Aamer Madhani, "Cleric al-Awlaki Dubbed 'bin Laden of the Internet,'" *USA Today,* September 20, 2011, at http://usatoday30.usatoday.com/news/nation/2010-08-25-1A_Awlaki25_CV_N.htm.

20. Adam Entous, Siobhan Gorman, and Julian E. Barnes, "U.S. Tightens Drone Rules," *Wall Street Journal,* November 4, 2011, at http://online.wsj.com/article/SB10001424052970204621904577013982672973836.html.

21. Adam Entous, Siobhan Gorman, and Julian E. Barnes, "U.S. Relaxes Drone Rules," *Wall Street Journal,* April 26, 2012, at http://online.wsj.com/article/SB10001424052702304723304577366251852418174.html.

22. Jo Becker and Scott Shane, "Secret 'Kill List' Proves a Test of Obama's Principles and Will," *New York Times,* May 29, 2012, at http://www.nytimes.com/2012/05/29/world/obamas-leadership-in-war-on-al-qaeda.html?pagewanted=all.

23. David Rohde, "The Obama Doctrine," *Foreign Policy,* March–April 2012, at http://www.foreignpolicy.com/articles/2012/02/27/the_obama_doctrine.

24. John Brennan, "The Efficacy and Ethics of U.S. Counterterrorism Strategy," April 30, 2012, at http://www.wilsoncenter.org/event/the-efficacy-and-ethics-us-counterterrorism-strategy.

25. Mark Lander, "Civilian Deaths Due to Drones Are Not Many, Obama Says," *New York Times,* January 20, 2012, at http://www.nytimes.com/2012/01/31/world/middleeast/civilian-deaths-due-to-drones-are-few-obama-says.html.

26. Owen Bowcott, "UN to Investigate Civilian Deaths from US Drone Strikes," *Guardian,* October 25, 2012, at http://www.guardian.co.uk/world/2012/oct/25/un-inquiry-us-drone-strikes.

27. Qasim Nauman, "Pakistan Condemns U.S. Drone Strikes," Reuters, June 4, 2012, at http://uk.reuters.com/article/2012/06/04/uk-pakistan-usa-drones-idUKBRE8530TF20120604.

28. Micah Zenko, *Reforming U.S. Drone Strike Policies,* Special Report no. 65 (New York: Council on Foreign Relations, January 2013), 15.

29. Dianne Feinstein, "Letters: Sen. Feinstein on Drone Strikes," *Los Angeles Times,* May 17, 2012, at http://articles.latimes.com/2012/may/17/opinion/la-le-0517-thursday-feinstein-drones-20120517.

30. Tim Starks, "Unmanned Oversight: How Congress Whiffed on Drones," *New Republic,* February 7, 2013.

31. Ken Dilanian, "Congress Zooms In on Drone Killings," *Los Angeles Times,* June 25, 2012, at http://articles.latimes.com/2012/jun/25/nation/la-na-drone-oversight-20120625.

32. Steven Aftergood, "Intelligence Oversight Steps Back from Public Accountability," January 2, 2013, at http://blogs.fas.org/secrecy/2013/01/public_accountability/.

33. Conor Friedersdorf, "Reports of Congressional Drone Oversight Are Greatly Exaggerated," *The Atlantic,* May 1, 2013, at http://www.theatlantic.com/politics/archive/2013/05/reports-of-congressional-drone-oversight-are-greatly-exaggerated/275451/.

34. Vicki Divoll, "Who Says You Can Kill Americans, Mr. President?" *New York Times,* January 16, 2013, at http://www.nytimes.com/2013/01/17/opinion/who-says-you-can-kill-americans-mr-president.html?_r=0.

35. "Rise of Drones: Unmanned Systems and the Future of War," in U.S. House of Representatives, *Hearing before the House Committee on Oversight and Government Reform,* 111th Cong., 2nd sess., March 23, 2010; "Rise of Drones II: The Legality of Unmanned Targeting," in U.S. House of Representatives, *Hearing before the House Committee on Oversight and Government Reform,* 111th Cong., 2nd sess., April 28, 2010.

36. Cong. Rec. H3278 (May 31, 2012).

37. Cong. Rec. H6078 (September 19, 2012).

38. Cong. Rec. H6377 (November 15, 2012). See also Cong. Rec. E1158 (June 27, 2012).

39. On Paul's previous war powers activity, see Ryan C. Hendrickson, *The Clinton Wars: The Constitution, Congress, and War Powers* (Nashville: Vanderbilt University Press, 2002), 151, 167.

40. For one of these letters, see http://democrats.judiciary.house.gov/sites/democrats.judiciary.house.gov/files/Conyers-Nadler-Scott120521.pdf.

41. Joe Wolverton, "Paul, Kucinich Drone Resolution Rejected by House Judiciary Committee," *New American,* December 18, 2012, at http://www.thenewamerican.com/usnews/congress/item/13971-paul-kucinich-drone-resolution-rejected-by-house-judiciary-committee. See a video of this committee hearing at http://www.youtube.com/watch?v=hQZyFRSP6QI.

42. Ken Dilanian, "Sen. Levin's Bid Boost to Drone Oversight Fails in Congress," *Los Angeles Times,* February 12, 2014, at http://www.latimes.com/world/worldnow/la-fg-wn-levin-drone-oversight-20140212,0,2114536.story#axzz2vafJt0S7.

3. Fighting Pirates on the Indian Ocean

1. Edith M. Lederer, "Somali Pirates Have Not Mounted a Successful Hijacking for Nearly a Year," *Christian Science Monitor,* May 3, 2013; Reuters, "Somalia: Successful Pirate Attacks Drop," *New York Times,* January 19, 2012, at http://www.nytimes.com/2012/01/20/world/africa/somalia-successful-pirate-attacks-drop

.html; Mark McDonald, "Record Number of Somali Pirate Attacks in 2009," *New York Times,* December 29, 2009, at http://www.nytimes.com/2009/12/30/world /africa/30piracy.html?_r=0.

2. Barack Obama, "Blocking Property of Certain Persons Contributing to the Conflict in Somalia," Exec. Order 13536, *Federal Register* 75, no. 72 (April 15, 2010): 19869–71.

3. U.S. Department of Defense, Office of the Assistant Secretary of State of Defense (Public Affairs), "DOD News Briefing with Vice Adm. Gortney from Bahrain," April 12, 2009, at http://www.defenselink.mil/transcripts/transcript .aspx?transcriptid=4400.

4. Headquarters United States Africa Command, April 1, 2010, at http://www .africom.mil/printStory.asp?art=4229, and Gordon Lubold, "USS Nicholas Captures Somali Pirates. What to Do with Them?" *Christian Science Monitor,* April 1, 2010.

5. "USS *Ashland* Captures Pirates," U.S. Navy press release, U.S. 5th Fleet Public Affairs, April 10, 2010, at http://www.navy.mil/search/display.asp?story_id=52519.

6. Quoted in Craig Whiltlock, "Marines Seize Ship from Pirates," *Washington Post,* September 10, 2010.

7. U.S. Department of Defense, "DOD News Briefing with Vice Adm. Fox via Telephone from Bahrain on Somali Piracy aboard the S/V Quest," February 22, 2011, at http://www.defense.gov/transcripts/transcript.aspx?transcriptid=4774; Keith Johnson, "Suspected Pirates Indicted in Yacht Killings," *Wall Street Journal,* March 11, 2011.

8. Alessandra Rizzo, "U.S. U.K. Forces Free Ship from Somali Pirates," *Navy Times,* October 11, 2011, at http://www.navytimes.com/article/20111011 /NEWS/110110306/U-S-U-K-forces-free-ship-from-Somali-pirates.

9. For Buchanan's book on her capture and rescue, see Jessica Buchanan and Erik Landemalm, with Anthony Flacco, *Impossible Odds: The Kidnapping of Jessica Buchanan and Her Dramatic Rescue by Seal Team Six* (New York: Atria Books, 2013).

10. C. J. Chivers, "For Iranians Waylaid by Pirates, U.S. to the Rescue," *New York Times,* January 6, 2012, at http://www.nytimes.com/2012/01/07/world/middleeast /for-iranians-held-by-pirates-us-to-the-rescue.html?pagewanted=all&_r=0.

11. Lauren Ploch, Christopher M. Blanchard, Ronald O'Rourke, R. Chuck Mason, and Rawle O. King, *Piracy off the Horn of Africa* (Washington, D.C.: Congressional Research Service, April 27, 2011), 25.

12. Ibid., 19–20.

13. On NATO's antipiracy efforts, see Nathan G. D. Garrett and Ryan C. Hendrickson, "NATO's Anti-piracy Operations: Strategic and Political Implications," *Atlantisch Perspectief* 33, no. 8 (2009): 9–13. On the EU, see *EU NAVFOR News,* at http://eunavfor.eu/.

14. James Madison, *Notes of Debates in the Federal Convention of 1787 Reported by James Madison* (1966; reprint, New York: Norton, 1987). Madison's Federalist Paper no. 42 mentions piracy but only in the context that the national government

will deal with this issue, which, as Madison maintains, was an improvement over the Articles of Confederation. See *The Federalist Papers* (New York: New American Library, 1961), 265–66.

15. Louis Fisher, *Presidential War Power,* 3rd ed. (Lawrence: University Press of Kansas, 2013), 33.

16. Ibid., 25.

17. Ibid., 24.

18. Robert F. Turner, *Repealing the War Powers Resolution* (Washington, D.C.: Brassey's, 1991), 60–61; Abram Sofaer, *War, Foreign Affairs, and Constitutional Power: The Origins* (Cambridge, Mass.: Ballinger, 1976), 212.

19. Francis D. Wormuth and Edwin B. Firmage, *To Chain the Dog of War: The War Power of Congress in History and Law,* 2nd ed. (Urbana: University of Illinois Press, 1989), 24.

20. Ibid., 64.

21. Quoted in ibid., 156.

22. United States Code, Title 33, chap. 7, § 381, quoted in Jennifer K. Elsea and Richard F. Grimmett, *Declarations of War and Authorizations for the Use of Military Force: Historical Background and Legal Implications* (Washington, D.C.: Congressional Research Service, March 17, 2011), 7.

23. James A. Wombwell, *The Long War against Piracy: Historical Trends,* Occasional Paper no. 32 (Ft. Leavenworth, Kans.: Combat Studies Institute Press, 2010), 48–49, 108.

24. Peter Lehr, "Maritime Piracy as a U.S. Foreign Policy Problem: The Case of the *Maersk Alabama,*" in *Contemporary Cases in U.S. Foreign Policy: From Terrorism to Trade,* 4th ed., ed. Ralph G. Carter (Washington, D.C.: Congressional Quarterly Press, 2011), 204.

25. Craig L. Symonds, *Navalists and Antinavalists: The Naval Policy Debate in the United States, 1785–1827* (Newark: University of Delaware Press, 1980), 231–35.

26. J. Peter Pham, "Anti-piracy, Adrift," *Journal of International Security Affairs* 18, no. 1 (2010), at http://www.securityaffairs.org/issues/2010/18/pham.php.

27. James Kraska, "Coalition Strategy and the Pirates of the Gulf of Aden and the Red Sea," *Comparative Strategy* 28, no. 3 (2009): 197–216.

28. For example, see U.S. House of Representatives, *Hearings before the Subcommittee on Africa, Global Health and Human Rights and the Subcommittee on Terrorism, Nonproliferation, and Trade,* 112th Cong., 1st sess., July 7, 2011; U.S. House of Representatives, *Assuring the Freedom of the Americans on the High Seas: The United States Response to Piracy: Hearing before the Subcommittee on Coast Guard and Maritime Transportation of the Committee on Transportation and Infrastructure,* 112th Cong., 1st sess., March 15, 2011.

29. For an excellent summary of U.S. and international governmental actions, including congressional committee hearings, taken to address pirates in Somalia, see http://ndu.libguides.com/content.php?pid=413715&sid=3380795.

30. U.S. House of Representatives, *International Piracy on the High Seas: Hearing*

before the Subcommittee on Coast Guard and Maritime Transportation of the Committee on Transportation and Infrastructure, 111th Cong., 1st sess., February 4, 2009, 15.

31. Cong. Rec. H4590–94 (April 22, 2009).

32. Cong. Rec. H4594 (April 22, 2009), for the quote from Jackson-Lee.

33. Cong. Rec. H4592 (April 22, 2009).

34. Ibid.

35. Quoted in George Will, "A Species Yet Not Extinct," *Newsweek,* October 1, 2006, at http://www.thedailybeast.com/newsweek/2006/10/01/a-species-yet-not-extinct.html.

36. U.S. House of Representatives, Armed Services Committee, "Skelton Urges President to Fight Piracy by Denying Safe Haven in Somalia," press release, April 14, 2009, at http://democrats.armedservices.house.gov/index.cfm/press-releases?ContentRecord_id=64e06846–2701–40fc-ac73–16641f7fde5d&ContentType_id=770e20a9=5d2a-40c5-a868-bcf7de9173a9&Group_id=fca18578-e10c-42e8=855a-020244bd590f&MonthDisplay=4&YearDisplay=2009.

37. Speaker of the House Nancy Pelosi, "Pelosi Statement on 'Rescue of Captain Richard Phillips,'" press statement, April 13, 2009, at http://www.democraticleader.gov/news/press/pelosi-statement-rescue-captain-richard-phillips.

38. U.S. House of Representatives, *Piracy against U.S. Flagged Vessels: Lessons Learned: Hearing before the Subcommittee on Coast Guard and Maritime Transportation of the Committee on Transportation and Infrastructure,* 111th Cong., 1st sess., May 20, 2009, 2.

39. Frank R. Lautenberg, "Piracy on the High Seas," May 5, 2009, at http://www.lautenberg.senate.gov/newsroom/Hearings/050509.cfm.

40. *Fox News,* "Ron Paul: How to Fight Somali Pirates," April 15, 2009, transcript at http://www.ronpaul.com/2009-04-16/ron-paul-how-to-fight-somali-pirates/.

41. Quoted in Erika Lovley, "Ron Paul's Plan to Fend Off Pirates," *Politico,* April 15, 2009, at http://www.politico.com/news/stories/0409/21245.html.

42. Cong. Rec. H11722 (October 23, 2009).

43. For example, see Cong. Rec. S1173 (March 3, 2011); S3150 (May 19, 2011).

44. Cong. Rec. S12410 (December 4, 2009).

45. Cong. Rec. H1595 (March 8, 2011).

46. Pham, "Anti-Piracy, Adrift"; Kraska, "Coalition Strategy."

47. For example, see statements made by Chairman LoBiondo, Rear Admiral Kevin S. Cook, and Principal Deputy Assistant Secretary of State Kurt Amend in *Assuring the Freedom of Americans on the High Seas: Hearing before the Subcommittee on Coast Guard and Maritime Transportation of the Committee on Transportation and Infrastructure,* 112th Cong., 1st sess., March 15, 2011, all of whom made nearly identical remarks regarding international law and piracy.

48. For more on Congress's role in UN missions, see Louis Fisher, "Sidestepping Congress: Presidents Acting under the UN and NATO," *Case Western Reserve Law Review* 47, no. 4 (1997): 1237; Louis Fisher, "The Korean War: On What Legal

Basis Did Truman Act?" *American Journal of International Law* 89, no. 1 (1995): 21; Michael J. Glennon, "The Constitution and Chapter VII of the United Nations Charter," *American Journal of International Law* 85, no. 1 (1991): 74–88; Matthew D. Berger, "Implementing a United Nations Security Council Resolution: The President's Power to Use Force with the Authorization of Congress," *Hastings International and Comparative Law Review* 15, no. 1 (1991): 83–109.

49. Shih Hsui-chua, "US Probe Testing Patience: Yang," *Taipei Times,* June 17, 2011.

50. Clifford D. May, "The Pirates of Somalia," *National Review Online,* March 3, 2011, at http://www.nationalreview.com/articles/261118/pirates-somalia-clifford-d-may; Max Boot, "Pirates, Then and Now," *Foreign Affairs* 88, no. 4 (2009): 94–107.

4. Obama's Military Strikes on Libya

1. Louis Fisher, "Parsing the War Power," *National Law Journal,* July 4, 2011, 50–51.

2. Office of the White House Press Secretary, "Press Conference by the President," June 29, 2011, at http://www.whitehouse.gov/the-press-office/2011/06/29/press-conference-president.

3. Barack Obama, "Remarks by the President on Libya," March 19, 2012, at http://www.whitehouse.gov/the-press-office/2011/03/19/remarks-president-libya.

4. Barack Obama, "Letter from the President Regarding the Commencement of Operations in Libya," March 21, 2011, at http://www.whitehouse.gov/the-press-office/2011/03/21/letter-president-regarding-commencement-operations-libya.

5. Press Secretary Jay Carney, Senior Director for Western Hemisphere Affairs Dan Restrepo, and Deputy National Security Advisor for Strategic Communications Ben Rhodes, press briefing, March 22, 2011, at http://www.whitehouse.gov/the-press-office/2011/03/22/press-briefing-press-secretary-jay-carney-senior-director-western-hemisp.

6. Cong. Rec. S1075–76 (March 1, 2011).

7. Louis Fisher, "Military Operations in Libya: No War? No Hostilities?" *Presidential Studies Quarterly* 42, no. 1 (2012): 184–85.

8. Caroline D. Krass, "Authority to Use Force in Libya," April 1, 2011, at http://www.justice.gov/sites/default/files/olc/opinions/2011/04/31/authority-military-use-in-libya.pdf.

9. Helene Cooper and David E. Sanger, "Target's Clear; Intent Is Not," *New York Times,* March 21, 2011.

10. Cong. Rec. S2110 (April 5, 2011); Charlie Savage, "Attack Renews Debate over Congressional Consent," *New York Times,* March 22, 2011.

11. Quoted in Jonathan Broder and Emily Cadei, "A Question of Authority," *Congressional Quarterly Weekly,* March 28, 2011, 670.

12. Rand Paul, "Obama's Unconstitutional Libya War," *Washington Times,* June 15, 2011; CNN, "Senator Rand Paul on Obama and Afghanistan," June 21, 2011,

transcript at http://situationroom.blogs.cnn.com/2011/06/21/rand-pauls-libya-resolution/; and David A. Fahrenthold, "Sen. Rand Paul: Congress Has Become 'an Irrelevancy' on War Powers," *Washington Post*, June 8, 2011, at http://www.washingtonpost.com/politics/sen-rand-paul-congress-has-become-an-irrelevancy-on-war-powers/2011/06/08/AGV2lyLH_story.html.

13. Cong. Rec. H2038 (March 29, 2011).

14. Ryan C. Hendrickson, *The Clinton Wars: The Constitution, Congress, and War Powers* (Nashville: Vanderbilt University Press, 2002), 18, 85, 138–59.

15. For an excellent summary of formal actions taken by the House and Senate on Libya, see Brien Hallett, "The 112th Congress, the War Powers Resolution, and the 2011 Libya Operation: A Normative Analysis of Functional and Organizational Incapacity," paper presented at the Annual Meeting of the Western Political Science Association, March 22–24, 2012, at http://wpsa.research.pdx.edu/meet/2012/hallett.pdf.

16. Cong. Rec. H3673 (May 25, 2011). Congressman Scott Garrett (R–N.J.) also called for a voice vote to indicate that nothing in the National Defense Authorization Act of 2012 authorized military force in Libya (Cong. Rec. H3614 [May 25, 2011]).

17. Dennis J. Kucinich, "The Seventh Annual Fritz B. Burns Lecture: The War Powers Resolution and Kosovo: The Power to Make War," *Loyola of Los Angeles Law Review* 34, no. 1 (2000): 61–69. See also Ryan C. Hendrickson, "Congress, War Powers, and the Judiciary: Restraining the Commander in Chief's Ability to Wage War," *Journal of African and International Law* 3, no. 3 (2010): 583–600.

18. Cong. Rec. H4023 (June 3, 2011).

19. Cong. Rec. H4000 (June 3, 2011).

20. Members of the group that filed suit in *Kucinich et al. v. Obama* included John Conyers (D–Mich.), Michael Capuano (D–Mass.), Walter Jones (R–N.C.), Howard Coble (R–N.C.), Tim Johnson (R–Ill.), Dan Burton (R–Ind.), Jimmy Duncan (R–Tenn.), Roscoe Bartlett (R–Md.), and Ron Paul (R–Tex.). Judge Reggie B. Walton in the United States District Court for the District of Columbia later dismissed this case, maintaining that it had no standing. See *Dennis Kucinich et al. Plaintiffs v. Barack Obama et al. Defendants*, Civil Action no. 11-1096 (October 20, 2011).

21. David Fahrenthold and Peter Finn, "Anger Ramps Up in Congress over Libya," *Washington Post*, June 19, 2011.

22. Charlie Savage and Mark Lander, "White House Defends Continuing U.S. Role in Libya Operation," *New York Times*, June 16, 2011.

23. Charlie Savage, "2 Top Lawyers Lose Argument on War Power," *New York Times*, June 18, 2011.

24. Joe Heck, "Heck Introduces Bill to End Operations in Libya," June 22, 2011, at http://heck.house.gov/press-release/heck-introduces-bill-end-operations-libya.

25. Cong. Rec. H4542 (June 24, 2011); Emily Cadei and Eugene Mulero, "House Rejects Defunding Libya Efforts," *Congressional Quarterly Weekly*, June 27, 2011, 1380.

26. For summaries of these actions, see Kim Geiger, "House Criticizes Libya Mission but Preserves Funding," *Los Angeles Times,* July 8, 2011, and Alexander C. Hart and Emily Cadei, "With Pro-Obama Libya Measure on Hold in Senate, House Weighs In," *Congressional Quarterly Weekly,* July 11, 2011, 1497.

27. Stephen R. Weissman, *A Culture of Deference: Congress's Failure of Leadership in Foreign Policy* (New York: Basic Books, 1995).

28. Jim Garamone, "Obama: Gadhafi's Death Marks End of Painful Era for Libya," American Forces Press Service, October 20, 2011, at http://www.defense .gov/News/NewsArticle.aspx?ID=65737.

29. Emily Cadei, "As Libya Rebellion Stalls, Congress Mulls Its Role," *Congressional Quarterly Weekly,* April 25, 2011, 908; David A. Fahrenthold, "Legislators Call Obama's Actions Illegal," *Washington Post,* May 26, 2011.

30. Congressman Timothy Johnson (R–Ill.), interviewed by the author, June 5, 2013, Champaign, Ill.

31. David A. Fahrenthold, "In the House, a Challenge on Libya," *Washington Post,* June 2, 2011; Jennifer Steinhauer and Charlie Savage, "House Sets Votes on Two Resolutions Critical of U.S. Role in Libya Conflict," *New York Times,* June 3, 2011.

32. Quoted in David A. Fahrenthold, "Senator Obama vs. President Obama," *Washington Post,* June 26, 2011.

33. Hendrickson, *The Clinton Wars,* 87–91.

34. Nancy E. Roman, "Close Vote on Troop Funding May Be a Sign of Clash to Come," *Washington Times,* December 15, 1995.

35. On Pelosi, see Steinhauer and Savage, "House Votes on Two Resolutions," and Mike Lillis, "Pelosi Backs Obama on Libya," June 16, 2011, at http://thehill .com/homenews/house/166843-pelosi-backs-obama-on-libya.

36. Cong. Rec. H4011 (June 3, 2011).

37. For example, see Gary W. Cox and William C. Terry, "Legislative Productivity in the 93d–105th Congresses," *Legislative Studies Quarterly* 33, no. 4 (2008): 603–18; John R. Hibbing, *Congressional Careers: Contours of Life in the U.S. House of Representatives* (Chapel Hill: University of North Carolina Press, 1991).

38. Gail Russell Chaddock, "Libya Intervention: Tea Party and Liberal Democrats Make Unusual Allies," *Christian Science Monitor,* March 21, 2011, at http:// www.csmonitor.com/USA/Politics/2011/0321/Libya-intervention-Tea-party-and-liberal-Democrats-make-unusual-allies. For more on war powers assertiveness from a "Tea Party–infused House," see Jennifer Steinhauer, "U.S. Mission Exposes Divisions in Congress and within G.O.P.," *New York Times,* June 22, 2011.

39. Hendrickson, *The Clinton Wars,* 167.

40. Dana Bash, "Republican Senators Press President on War Powers Deadline," *CNN Politics,* May 18, 2011, at http://politicalticker.blogs.cnn.com/2011/05/18 /republican-senators-press-president-on-war-powers-deadline/.

41. Jennifer Steinhauer, "Kerry and McCain Introduce Libya Resolution," *New York Times Blog,* June 21, 2011, at http://thecaucus.blogs.nytimes.com/2011/06/21 /kerry-and-mccain-introduce-libya-resolution/?_php=true&_type=blogs&_r=0.

42. Quoted in Geiger, "House Criticizes Libya Mission."

43. Cadei, "As Libya Rebellion Stalls," 908.

44. Quoted in Josh Rogin, "Senate Braces for Long Libya Debate," *Washington Post,* June 23, 2011.

45. Quoted in Jonathan Broder and Seth Stern, "The Power in a Word," *Congressional Quarterly Weekly,* June 27, 2011, 1370.

46. U.S. Senate, *Libya and War Powers: Hearings before the Foreign Relations Committee,* 112th Cong., 1st sess., June 28, 2011, 25–28, at http://www.fas.org/irp/congress/2011_hr/libya.pdf. In addition, two constitutional law experts, Louis Fisher and Peter Spiro, provided opening statements regarding President Obama's actions. However, nearly all questions and remarks from committee members were directed toward Harold Koh, who presented the administration's legal claims. See http://www.foreign.senate.gov/hearings/hearing/?id=3c07358f-5056-a032–5263-cbae117ccfb9.

47. Felicia Sonmez, "Kerry, McCain to Introduce Bipartisan Resolution on Libya," *Washington Post,* June 21, 2011, at http://www.washingtonpost.com/blogs/2chambers/post/kerry-mccain-to-introduce-bipartisan-libya-resolution/2011/06/21/AGlabReH_blog.html.

48. On Levin, see Jonathan Broder, "Divided over a Stealth War," *Congressional Quarterly Weekly,* April 4, 2011, 754.

49. Charlie Savage and Jennifer Steinhauer, "In House, Challenges over Policy on Libya," *New York Times,* June 23, 2011.

50. Fahrenthold and Finn, "Anger Ramps Up in Congress over Libya."

51. On Lugar's role on NATO enlargement in the 1990s, see James M. Goldgeier, *Not Whether but When: The U.S. Decision to Enlarge NATO* (Washington, D.C.: Brookings Institution Press, 1999), 35.

52. Lugar managed to gain "voice votes" in the Foreign Relations Committee that expressed the committee's view that the United States was engaged in hostilities; however, such votes do not require a member of Congress to go on record with his or her actual position. See Emily Cadei and Joanna Anderson, "President Wins Panel's Support on Libya," *Congressional Quarterly Weekly,* July 4, 2011, 1441.

53. On Amash's independence witnessed early in his House career, see Jennifer Steinhauer, "No, No, No, No, No, No, No, No, No, No, No, No," *New York Times,* April 15, 2011.

54. It is notable that even in cases where Congress did in recent times authorize the use of force, including the Gulf War in 1991 and Afghanistan in 2001, presidents still maintained that they did not need congressional authorization to use force. See Louis Fisher, *Presidential War Power,* 3rd ed. (Lawrence: University Press of Kansas, 2013).

55. Mark Mazzetti and Eric Schmitt, "C.I.A. Agents in Libya Aid Airstrikes and Meet Rebels," *New York Times,* March 30, 2011, at http://www.nytimes.com/2011/03/31/world/africa/31intel.html.

56. Quoted in Jonathan Broder and Seth Stern, "The Power in a Word," *Congressional Quarterly Weekly,* June 27, 2011, 1370.

5. The Hunt for Joseph Kony

1. On Kony and the LRA in general, see Jeroen Adam, Bruno Decordier, Kristof Titeca, and Koen Vlassenroot, "In the Name of the Father? Christian Militantism in Tripura, Northern Uganda, and Ambon," *Studies in Conflict and Terrorism* 30, no. 11 (2007): 963–83; Susan McKay, "Girls as 'Weapons of Terror' in Northern Uganda and Sierra Leone Rebel Fighting Forces," *Studies in Conflict and Terrorism* 28, no. 5 (2005): 385–97; Adam Branch, "Neither Peace nor Justice: Political Violence and Peasantry in Northern Uganda, 1986–1998," *African Studies Quarterly* 8, no. 2 (2005): 1–31; Anthony Vinci, "The Strategic Use of Fear by the Lord's Resistance Army," *Small Wars and Insurgencies* 16, no. 3 (2005): 360–81.

2. Barack Obama, "Letter from the President to the Speaker of the House of Representatives and the President Pro Tempore of the Senate regarding the Lord's Resistance Army," Office of the White House Press Secretary, October 14, 2011, at http://www.whitehouse.gov/the-press-office/2011/10/14/letter-president-speaker-house-representatives-and-president-pro-tempore. Precise details on the kind of U.S. Special Forces deployed in Africa are limited, though some sources indicate the presence of U.S. Army Special Forces. See *Daily Mail* (United Kingdom), "U.S. Special Forces Close In on Jungle Hideout of Ugandan Warlord Joseph Kony," April 30, 2012, at http://www.dailymail.co.uk/news/article-2137144/Kony-2012-U-S-special-forces-hunt-warlord-remote-Ugandan-village.html, and Rajiv Chandrasekaran, "Kony 2013: U.S. Quietly Intensifies Effort to Help African Troops Capture Infamous Warlord," *Washington Post,* October 28, 2013, at http://www.washingtonpost.com/world/national-security/kony-2013-us-quietly-intensifies-effort-to-help-african-troops-capture-infamous-warlord/2013/10/28/74db9720-3cb3-11e3-b6a9-da62c264f40e_story.html.

3. Quote in Jake Tapper, "Activists React to President Sending Troops to Africa," *ABC News,* October 17, 2011, at http://abcnews.go.com/blogs/politics/2011/10/activists-react-to-president-sending-troops-to-africa/. The LRA Disarmament Act's language allowed the president to provide "political, economic, military, and intelligence support for viable multilateral efforts to protect civilians from the Lord's Resistance Army, to apprehend or remove Joseph Kony and his top commanders from the battlefield." See Obama, "Letter from the President to the Speaker of the House or Representatives and the President Pro Tempore of the Senate regarding the Lord's Resistance Army."

4. David Mayhew, *Congress: The Electoral Connection* (New Haven, Conn.: Yale University Press, 1974).

5. See, for example, Trevor Rubenzer, "Campaign Contributions and US Foreign Policy Outcomes: An Analysis of Cuban-American Interests," *American Journal of Political Science* 55, no. 1 (2011): 105–16; Ellen A. Cutrone and Benjamin O. Fordham, "Commerce and Imagination: The Sources of Concern about International Human Rights in the US Congress," *International Studies Quarterly* 54, no. 3 (2010): 633–55; Mark Souva and David Rohde, "Elite Differences and Partisanship

in Congressional Foreign Policy, 1975–1996," *Political Research Quarterly* 60, no. 1 (2007): 113–23; Bryan W. Marshall and Brandon C. Prins, "The Pendulum of Congressional Power: Agenda Change, Partisanship, and Demise of Post–World War II Foreign Policy Consensus," *Congress and the Presidency* 29, no. 2 (2002): 195–212.

6. See, for example, Ralph G. Carter and James M. Scott, *Choosing to Lead: Congressional Foreign Policy Entrepreneurs* (Durham, N.C.: Duke University Press, 2009); C. James Delaet, Charles M. Rowling, and James M. Scott, "Partisanship, Ideology, and Weapons of Mass Destruction in the Post–Cold War Congress: The Chemical Weapons and Comprehensive Test Ban Cases," *Illinois Political Science Review* 11, no. 1 (2007): 2–34; Robert David Johnson, *Congress and the Cold War* (New York: Cambridge University Press, 2006); David Auerswald and Forrest Matlzman, "Policymaking through Advice and Consent: Treaty Considerations by the United States Senate," *Journal of Politics* 65, no. 4 (2003): 1097–1110.

7. Barry C. Burden, *Personal Roots of Representation* (Princeton, N.J.: Princeton University Press, 2007).

8. James M. McCormick and Neil J. Mitchell, "Commitments, Transnational Interests, and Congress: Who Joins the Congressional Human Rights Caucus?" *Political Research Quarterly* 60, no. 4 (2007): 579–92; Susan Webb Hammond, *Congressional Caucuses in National Policy Making* (Baltimore: Johns Hopkins University Press, 1998); Ralph G. Carter, James M. Scott, and Charles M. Rowling, "Setting a Course: Congressional Foreign Policy Entrepreneurs in Post World War II U.S. Foreign Policy," *International Studies Perspectives* 5, no. 3 (2004): 278–99.

9. Alexis Arieff and Lauren Ploch, *The Lord's Resistance Army: The U.S. Response* (Washington, D.C.: Congressional Research Service, April 11, 2012), 4–5.

10. David Halberstam, *War in a Time of Peace: Bush, Clinton, and the Generals* (New York: Scribner's, 2001), 265.

11. Charles D. Allen, "Assessing the Army Profession," *Parameters* 41, no. 4 (2011): 75; Andrew J. Bacevich, *The Limits of Power: The End of American Exceptionalism* (New York: Holt, 2008); Richard N. Haass, "The Age of Nonpolarity," *Foreign Affairs* 87, no. 3 (2008): 44–56.

12. See the video at http://video.google.com/videoplay?docid=316679775 3930210643#.

13. Sally Deneen, "Making a Difference—Invisible Children," *Success,* January 6, 2009, at http://www.success.com/articles/523-making-a-difference-invisible-children.

14. Bruce Wilson, "Kony 2012, Invisible Children, and the Religious Right: The Evidence," *Talk to Action,* April 16, 2012, at http://www.talk2action.org/story/2012/4/16/223727/559.

15. Critics noted that the video contained several mistakes. Among the criticisms, see Michael Wilkerson, "Guest Post: Joseph Kony Is Not in Uganda (and Other Complicated Things)," March 7, 2012, at http://blog.foreignpolicy.com/posts/2012/03/07/guest_post_joseph_kony_is_not_in_uganda_and_other_complicated_things.

16. Gilad Lotan, "[Data Viz] KONY2012: See How Invisible Networks Helped

a Campaign Capture the World's Attention," *Socialflow,* March 24, 2012, at http://giladlotan.com/2012/03/data-viz-kony2012-see-how-invisible-networks-helped-a-campaign-capture-the-worlds-attention/.

17. Michael Poffenberger, Resolve Uganda, telephone interview by the author, June 5, 2012.

18. Ekaterina Strekalova, "American Youth Take on the Cause of Child Soldiers," June 24, 2009, at http://www.unausa.org/Page.aspx?pid=1332.

19. Shea Yarborough, "Senator Gives In to Activists," *NT Daily,* March 10, 2010, at http://www.ntdaily.com/?p=7450.

20. Quote from Michael Poffenberger, Resolve Uganda, telephone interview by the author, May 17, 2012; see also Meghna J. Raj, former government relations associate to Enough Project, email correspondence with the author, July 1, 2012.

21. Cong. Rec. H3413 (May 12, 2010).

22. Quoted in John Prendergast, with Don Cheadle, *The Enough Movement: Fighting to End Africa's Worst Human Rights Crimes* (New York: Three Rivers Press, 2010), 167.

23. Cong. Rec. S5616 (May 19, 2009).

24. Cong. Rec. H5866 (May 20, 2009).

25. Cong. Rec. E864 (May 18, 2010).

26. Cong. Rec. H3411 (May 12, 2010).

27. Cong. Rec. H3415 (May 12, 2010).

28. Sarah Margon, "Viewpoint: A Partial Defense of Invisible Children's Kony 2012 Campaign," *ThinkProgress,* March 8, 2012, at http://thinkprogress.org/security/2012/03/08/440851/defense-kony-invisible-children/.

29. Stephen Zunes and Ben Terrall, "East Timor: Reluctant Support for Self-Determination," in *Contemporary Cases in U.S. Foreign Policy,* ed. Ralph G. Carter (Washington, D.C.: Congressional Quarterly Press, 2002), 1–30.

30. Cong. Rec. S8846 (September 16, 2008); S5616 (May 19, 2009); S822 (February 26, 2010).

31. Cong. Rec. S3067 (March 12, 2009).

32. Sarah Margon, former senior foreign-policy staff assistant to Senator Russ Feingold, telephone interview by the author, May 31, 2012.

33. As noted in Prendergast, with Cheadle, *The Enough Movement,* 156.

34. On Feingold's relationship with Coburn, see the Margon interview, May 31, 2012; on Feingold's more general staff activism, see both the Margon interview and the Poffenberger interview, May 17, 2012.

35. MSNBC, "Sen. James M. Inhofe, R-OKLA. Is Interviewed on MSNBC," March 15, 2012, transcript at http://www.msnbc.msn.com/id/46762101/ns/msnbc_tv-rachel_maddow_show/t/rachel-maddow-show-thursday-march/.

36. National Public Radio, "Family: Fundamentalism, Friends in High Places," July 1, 2009, transcript at http://www.npr.org/templates/story/story.php?storyId=106115324.

37. Quoted in Chris Casteel, "U.S. Senator Jim Inhofe's Trips to Africa

Called a 'Jesus Thing,'" NEWSOK, December 21, 2008, at http://newsok
.com/u.s.-senator-jim-inhofes-trips-to-africa-called-a-jesus-thing/article/3331838.

38. Ibid.

39. MSNBC, "Sen. James M. Inhofe, R-OKLA."

40. U.S. Senate, Armed Services Committee, *Hearing to Receive Testimony on United States Southern Command, United States Northern Command, United States Africa Command, and United States Transportation Command,* 111th Cong., 1st sess., March 17, 2009, 20; Cong. Rec. S8920 (September 17, 2008).

41. Poffenberger interview, May 17, 2012.

42. Quotes from Michael Luo, "In Crowded G.O.P. Field, a Lesser-Known Hopes to Capitalize on the Issues," *New York Times,* March 12, 2007.

43. Brownback also served as a co-sponsor with Senators Dick Durbin (D–Ill.) and Russ Feingold (D–Wisc.) on the Congo Conflict Minerals Act, which calls upon greater oversight of the international trade that may benefit groups that carry out human rights abuses in eastern Congo. See Gus Constantine, "Congo, a Country That's Broken," *Washington Times,* September 8, 2009. Others who may have been motivated by a Christian evangelical motive to address Kony include Senator Johnny Isakson (R–Ga.), who was willing to support this issue but is not otherwise supportive of issues that can be characterized as left-leaning human rights concerns (Raj, email correspondence, July 1, 2012).

44. Michael Barone, with Richard E. Cohen and Grant Ujifusa, *The Almanac of American Politics 2010* (Washington, D.C.: National Journal Group, 2009), 739.

45. Margon interview, May 31, 2012.

46. Prendergast, with Cheadle, *The Enough Movement,* 167.

47. Strekalova, "American Youth Take on the Cause of Children Soldiers."

48. Poffenberger interview, May 17, 2012.

49. Office of Congressman Ed Royce, "Media Advisory: Rep. Royce, Invisible Children Push 'Stop Kony' Legislation at Friday Press Conference," March 15, 2012, at http://royce.house.gov/News/DocumentSingle.aspx?DocumentID=284955.

50. Margon interview, May 31, 2012.

51. Ibid.

52. A full list of co-sponsors is given at http://www.theresolve.org/pages/list-of-congressional-cosponsors.

53. Cong. Rec. S822 (February 26, 2010).

54. U.S. Department of State, "Terror Exclusion List," December 29, 2004, at http://www.state.gov/j/ct/rls/other/des/123086.htm.

55. U.S. Department of State, "The Lord's Resistance Army: Fact Sheet," March 23, 2012, at http://www.state.gov/r/pa/prs/ps/2012/03/186734.htm.

56. Gallup Poll, "Terrorism Tops Americans' International Concerns," April 6, 2009, at http://www.gallup.com/video/117298/Terrorism-Tops-Americans-International-Concerns.aspx.

57. Gallup Poll, "Federal Debt, Terrorism, Considered Top Threats to U.S.,"

June 4, 2010, at http://www.gallup.com/poll/139385/Federal-Debt-Terrorism-Considered-Top-Threats.aspx.

58. Cong. Rec. H3413 (May 12, 2010).

59. Cong. Rec. H3411 (May 12, 2010).

60. Cong. Rec. H3415 (May 12, 2010).

61. Jeffrey Gentleman and Eric Schmitt, "U.S. Aided a Failed Plan to Rout Uganda Rebels," *New York Times,* February 6, 2009.

62. Poffenberger interview, May 17, 2012.

63. Ibid.

64. Cong. Rec. H3409 (May 12, 2010).

65. Cong. Rec. S1409–12 (March 10, 2010); H3409–16 (May 12, 2010).

66. Peter Grier, "Why Did Rush Limbaugh Defend Joseph Kony and the Lord's Resistance Army?" *Christian Science Monitor,* March 9, 2012, at http://www.csmonitor.com/USA/Elections/Vox-News/2012/0309/Why-did-Rush-Limbaugh-defend-Joseph-Kony-and-Lord-s-Resistance-Army-video.

67. "Bachmann Talks Foreign Policy with Glenn Beck: Africa," *Examiner,* November 22, 2011, at http://www.examiner.com/article/bachmann-talks-foreign-policy-with-glenn-beck-africa.

68. "CNN Interview with John McCain," October 16, 2011, at http://transcripts.cnn.com/TRANSCRIPTS/1110/16/sotu.01.html.

69. David P. Forsythe, *Human Rights in International Relations,* 3rd ed. (Cambridge: Cambridge University Press, 2012), 258.

70. Poffenberger interview, June 5, 2012.

71. Raj, email correspondence, July 1, 2012.

72. Margon interview, May 31, 2012.

73. Poffenberger interview, June 5, 2012. See also Prendergast, with Cheadle, *The Enough Movement.*

74. Chandrasekaran, "Kony 2013."

6. Senators Kerry and McCain

1. Kerry earned the Silver Star and the Bronze Star and was awarded three Purple Hearts for his military activities in Vietnam.

2. John Kerry, testimony to the U.S. Senate, Committee on Foreign Relations, *Legislative Proposals Relating to the War in Southeast Asia,* 92nd Cong., 1st sess., April 22, 1971.

3. Cong. Rec. 5130 (March 18, 1986).

4. Cong. Rec. S14332 (October 2, 1990).

5. Cong. Rec. 24616 (September 14, 1994).

6. David P. Forsythe, *The Politics of International Law: U.S. Foreign Policy Reconsidered* (Boulder, Colo.: Lynne Rienner, 1990), 63–88.

7. George P. Shultz, *Turmoil and Triumph: My Years as Secretary of State* (New York: Scribner's, 1993), 334–35.

8. Brett M. Hall, Ryan C. Hendrickson, and Nathan M. Polak, "Diversionary American Military Actions? American Military Strikes on Grenada and Iraq," *Comparative Strategy* 32, no. 1 (2013): 35–51.

9. Michael Rubner, "The Reagan Administration, the 1973 War Powers Resolution, and the Invasion of Grenada," *Political Science Quarterly* 100 (1985–1986): 627–47.

10. Cong. Rec. 23933 (October 7, 1993).

11. Ronald Reagan, "Letter to the Speaker of the House of Representatives and the President Pro Tempore of the Senate of the United States on the United States Air Strike against Libya," *Public Papers of the Presidents,* April 6, 1986, 478.

12. Pat Towell, "After the Raid on Libya, New Questions on the Hill," *Congressional Quarterly Weekly,* April 19, 1986, 839.

13. Cong. Rec. 23933 (October 7, 1993).

14. Kerry had voted for a "Sense of the Senate" resolution on October 5, 1989, which encouraged President Bush to restore the constitutional government in Panama, but such a resolution is not equivalent to a declaration of war and does not have legally binding status. See Cong. Rec. S12690 (October 5, 1989).

15. Cong. Rec. 19572–73 (September 6, 1989).

16. Cong. Rec. 1011 (January 12, 1991).

17. Cong. Rec. 1829 (January 17, 1991).

18. Cong. Rec. 5925 (March 13, 1991).

19. Cong. Rec. 25243 (October 19, 1993).

20. Ryan C. Hendrickson, *The Clinton Wars: The Constitution, Congress, and War Powers* (Nashville: Vanderbilt University Press, 2002), 67.

21. Cong. Rec. 24615–16 (September 14, 1994).

22. Cong. Rec. 1780 (February 9, 1994); Cong. Rec. S3110 (March 23, 1999).

23. Cong. Rec. H10095 (September 5, 1996); Adrianne Flynne, "GOP Senators Displeased at Being in the Dark on Iraq," *Arizona Republic,* September 6, 1996.

24. Cong. Rec. S9937 (September 5, 1996).

25. Interviewed on *ABC This Week,* February 22, 1998, transcript no. 98022203-j12.

26. See Louis Fisher, "Military Action against Iraq," *Presidential Studies Quarterly* 28, no. 4 (1998): 796.

27. Hendrickson, *The Clinton Wars,* esp. chap. 7.

28. Cong. Rec. S9424 (September 14, 2001).

29. Cong. Rec. S9416 (September 14, 2001).

30. Cong. Rec. S9423 (September 14, 2001).

31. Cong. Rec. S9417 (September 14, 2001).

32. See Nancy Kassop, "The War Power and Its Limit," *Presidential Studies Quarterly* 33, no. 3 (2003): 509–29.

33. David Abramowitz, "The President, the Congress, and Use of Force: Legal and Political Considerations in Authorizing Use of Force against International Terrorism," *Harvard International Law Journal* 43, no. 1 (2002): 71–82.

34. John Kerry, "We Still Have a Choice on Iraq," *New York Times,* September 6, 2002.

35. Mike Allen and Juliet Eilperin, "Bush Aides Say Iraq War Needs No Hill Vote," *Washington Post,* August 26, 2002.

36. Cong. Rec. S10175 (October 9, 2002).

37. Chuck Hagel, with Peter Kaminsky, *America: Our Next Chapter; Tough Questions, Straight Answers* (New York: HarperCollins, 2008), 54–55.

38. Louis Fisher, "Deciding on War against Iraq: Institutional Failures," *Political Science Quarterly* 118, no. 3 (2003): 389–410.

39. Michael Keller, "John Kerry's Flip Flops," n.d., at http://www.michaelkeller .com/news/news816.htm.

40. The court dismissed the case on grounds that the question posed by the plaintiffs was a "political question" and thus not appropriate for consideration. See *John Doe I et al., Plaintiffs, v. President George W. Bush and Secretary of Defense Donald H. Rumsfeld,* United States District Court for the District of Massachusetts (February 27, 2003).

41. Cong. Rec. 26118 (September 28, 1983).

42. Donna H. Henry, "Notes: The War Powers Resolution: A Tool for Balancing Power through Negotiation," *Virginia Law Review* 70 (1984): 1051. See also Louis Fisher, *Presidential War Power,* 3rd ed. (Lawrence: University Press of Kansas, 2013), 160–61.

43. Cong. Rec. 26118 (September 28, 1983).

44. Ibid.

45. Cong. Rec. 29994 (October 31, 1983).

46. Fisher, *Presidential War Power,* 162.

47. Shultz, *Turmoil and Triumph,* 334–35.

48. William Welch, "McCain Says Dukakis Is Weak on Defense," Associated Press, August 16, 1988; Cong. Rec. S473 (February 9, 1998).

49. Welch, "McCain Says Dukakis Is Weak on Defense."

50. Cong. Rec. 27183 (October 9, 1987).

51. Ibid.

52. Ibid.

53. Cong. Rec. S473 (February 9,1998).

54. Cong. Rec. S11548 (August 2, 1990).

55. Cong. Rec. S966 (January 17, 1991).

56. Senator John Sidney McCain III, "Remarks on Kosovo and NATO," interview, Center for Strategic and International Studies, April 13, 1999.

57. Cong. Rec. S10663 (August 5, 1994).

58. Cong. Rec. S10655 (August 5, 1994).

59. Cong. Rec. S10656 (August 5, 1994).

60. Ibid.

61. Cong. Rec. S10666–67 (August 5, 1994).

62. Cong. Rec. S10667 (August 5, 1994).

63. Ibid.

64. Ibid.

65. Cong. Rec. S18546 (December 13, 1995).

66. Cong. Rec. S4611 (May 4, 1999).

67. Cong. Rec. S4612 (May 4, 1999).

68. Cong. Rec. S4616 (May 4, 1999).

69. R. W. Apple Jr., "On Two Fronts: The Overview," *New York Times,* December 18, 1998.

70. Adrianne Flynn, "GOP Senators Displeased at Being in the Dark on Iraq," *Arizona Republic,* September 6, 1996.

71. Adam Nagourney, "Raid on Iraq: The GOP," *New York Times,* September 4, 1996; R. W. Apple Jr., "Raid on Iraq: The Implications," *New York Times,* September 5, 1996.

72. McCain, "Remarks on Kosovo and NATO."

73. Steven Lee Meyers, "After the Attacks: The Overview," *New York Times,* August 23, 1998.

74. Ryan C. Hendrickson and Frédérick Gagnon, "The United States vs. Terrorism: Clinton, Bush, and Osama Bin Laden," in *Contemporary Cases in U.S. Foreign Policy: From Terrorism to Trade,* 3rd ed., ed. Ralph Carter (Washington, D.C.: Congressional Quarterly Press, 2007), 1–24.

75. Cong. Rec. S9417 (September 14, 2001).

76. Cong. Rec. S9422 (September 14, 2001).

77. Cong. Rec. S9416–17 (September 14, 2001).

78. Cong. Rec. S10233 (October 10, 2002).

79. Cong. Rec. S10235 (October 10, 2002).

80. Cong. Rec. S10167 (October 9, 2002).

81. Cong. Rec. S10249 (October 10, 2002).

82. Cong. Rec. S10250 (October 10, 2002).

83. Cong. Rec. S10191 (October 9, 2002).

84. Ibid.

85. Cong. Rec. S10254–55 (October 10, 2002).

86. Fisher, "Deciding on War against Iraq."

7. Syria and Beyond

1. Stephen R. Weissman, *A Culture of Deference: Congress's Failure of Leadership in Foreign Policy* (New York: Basic Books, 1995).

2. For example, see William G. Howell and Jon C. Pevehouse, *While Dangers Gather: Congressional Checks on Presidential War Powers* (Princeton, N.J.: Princeton University Press, 2007).

3. Barack Obama, "Remarks to the White House Press Corps," August 20, 2012, at http://www.whitehouse.gov/the-press-office/2012/08/20/remarks-president-white-house-press-corps.

4. Office of the White House Press Secretary, "Government Assessment of

the Syrian Government's Use of Chemical Weapons on August 21, 2013," August 30, 2013, at http://www.whitehouse.gov/the-press-office/2013/08/30/government-assessment-syrian-government-s-use-chemical-weapons-august-21.

5. Ben Hubbard, "Signs of Chemical Attack Detailed by Aid Group," *New York Times*, August 24, 2013, at http://www.nytimes.com/2013/08/25/world/middleeast/syria-updates.html.

6. Michael R. Gordon and Mark Lander, "Kerry Cites Clear Evidence of Chemical Weapons Use in Syria," *New York Times*, August 26, 2013, at http://www.nytimes.com/2013/08/27/world/middleeast/syria-assad.html?_r=0.

7. Peter Baker and Michael R. Gordon, "Kerry Becomes Chief Advocate for U.S. Attack," *New York Times*, August 30, 2013, at http://www.nytimes.com/2013/08/31/world/middleeast/john-kerry-syria.html.

8. John Kerry, "Statement on Syria," August 30, 2013, at http://www.state.gov/secretary/remarks/2013/08/213668.htm, emphasis added.

9. Chuck Hagel, with Peter Kaminsky, *America: Our Next Chapter; Tough Questions, Straight Answers* (New York: HarperCollins, 2008), 38, 58.

10. Quoted in Alan Cowell, Steven Erlanger, and Rick Gladstone, "Momentum Builds for Military Strike in Syria," *New York Times on the Web*, August 28, 2013, at http://www.nytimes.com/2013/08/28/world/middleeast/britain-preparing-contingency-plan-for-intervention-in-syria-officials-say.html?_r=0.

11. Shaskank Bengali, Paul Richter, and David S. Cloud, "The Syria Crisis: News Analysis: White House's U-turn Gamble," *Los Angeles Times*, September 1, 2013; Scott Wilson, "In the Oval Office, a Debate about Whether to Involve Lawmakers," *Washington Post*, September 1, 2013.

12. Barack Obama, "Statement by the President on Syria," August 31, 2013, at http://www.whitehouse.gov/the-press-office/2013/08/31/statement-president-syria.

13. See Jeffrey S. Lantis and Eric Moskowitz, "Executive Decisions and Preventive War: Strategies of Intervention and Withdrawal in Iraq (2003–2011)," in *Contemporary Cases in U.S. Foreign Policy: From Terrorism to Trade*, 5th ed., ed. Ralph G. Carter (Washington, D.C.: Congressional Quarterly Press, 2014), 79–80.

14. Cong. Rec. S3101 (March 23, 1999).

15. See also Ryan C. Hendrickson, *The Clinton Wars: The Constitution, Congress, and War Powers* (Nashville: Vanderbilt University Press, 2002).

16. Ed O'Keefe, "Amash: Syria Strike 'Unquestionably Unconstitutional' without Congressional Approval," *Washington Post*, August 27, 2013, at http://www.washingtonpost.com/blogs/post-politics/wp/2013/08/27/amash-syria-strike-unquestionably-unconstitutional-without-congressional-approval/.

17. Press Office of Speaker Boehner, "Boehner Seeks Answers from President Obama on Syria," August 28, 2013, at http://www.speaker.gov/press-release/boehner-seeks-answers-president-obama-syria.

18. Scott Rigell, "Rigell Leads Bipartisan Effort Urging President Obama to Get Congressional Approval before Striking Syria," August 28, 2013, at http://rigell.house.gov/news/documentsingle.aspx?DocumentID=347024.

19. Ibid.

20. Tom Howell Jr. and Stephen Dinan, "Republicans Implore Obama: Get Off the Sidelines on Syria Issue; U.N. to Visit Attack Site," *Washington Times*, August 25, 2013, at http://www.washingtontimes.com/news/2013/aug/25/mccain-graham-call-military-action-syria-chemical-/?page=all.

21. Quoted in David Savage, "Members of Congress Call for Syria Strike," *Los Angeles Times*, August 26, 2013, at http://www.washingtontimes.com/news/2013/aug/25/mccain-graham-call-military-action-syria-chemical-/?page=all.

22. Quoted in Michael A. Memoli, "Members of Congress Press for Vote Ahead of Possible Syria Strike," *Los Angeles Times*, August 27, 2013, at http://articles.latimes.com/2013/aug/27/news/la-pn-congress-vote-syria-strike-20130827.

23. Savage, "Members of Congress Call for Syria Strike"; Michael R. Gordon and Thom Shanker, "In Hearing, House Panel Seems Split on Syria Strike," *New York Times*, September 4, 2013, at http://www.nytimes.com/2013/09/05/world/middleeast/in-hearing-house-panel-seems-split-on-syria-strike.html?_r=0.

24. Chris Cillizza, "Is the Syria Resolution Nancy Pelosi's Great Test? Should It Be?" *Washington Post*, September 5, 2013, at http://www.washingtonpost.com/blogs/the-fix/wp/2013/09/05/is-the-syria-resolution-nancy-pelosis-greatest-test-should-it-be/.

25. Aaron Blake and David Nakamura, "Boehner and Cantor Will Support Syria Strike," *Washington Post*, September 3, 2013, at http://www.washingtonpost.com/blogs/post-politics/wp/2013/09/03/boehner-and-cantor-will-support-syria-strike/.

26. Michael Scherer and Alex Altman, "Q&A: Nancy Pelosi Talks about Syria with TIME," *TIME: Swampland*, September 5, 2013, at http://swampland.time.com/2013/09/05/qa-nancypelosi-talks-about-syria-attack-with-time/; Southern Maryland News Net, "Hoyer Statement on Syria," September 3, 2013, at http://smnewsnet.com/archives/78765; Mario Trujillo, "Hoyer: Obama Does Not Need Approval from Congress to Strike Syria's Assad," *The Hill*, September 13, 2013, at http://thehill.com/blogs/global-affairs/middle-east-north-africa/322075-hoyer-obama-doesnt-need-congressional-approval-for-syria-strike; NBCLatino, "Rep. Xavier Becerra Supports Limited US Strike in Syria: 'Morally Irresponsible for Us Not to Do Something,'" September 5, 2013, at http://nbclatino.com/2013/09/05/rep-xavier-becerra-supports-us-strike-in-syria-it-would-be-morally-irresponsible-for-us-not-to-do-something/.

27. Jared A. Farole, Colleen McCain Nelson, and Patrick O'Connor, "Key Lawmakers Back Obama on Syria Strike," *Wall Street Journal*, September 3, 2013, at http://online.wsj.com/news/articles/SB10001424127887324432404579052882138751904.

28. David Eldridge and Stephen Dinan, "Rep. 'Buck' McKeon: Obama Can Win Syria Votes by Undoing Sequester Cuts," *Washington Times*, September 8, 2013, at http://www.washingtontimes.com/news/2013/sep/8/rep-buck-mckeon-obama-can-win-syria-votes-undoing-/?page=all.

29. Brett Logiurato, "The Vote on Syria Is Shaping Up to Be a Full-Fledged Disaster for Obama," *Business Week*, September 6, 2013, at http://www.businessinsider.com/syria-vote-whip-count-house-senate-obama-2013-9.

30. Anthony Faiola, "British Prime Minister David Cameron Loses Parliamentary Vote on Syria Military Strike," *Washington Post,* August 29, 2013, at http://www.washingtonpost.com/world/europe/british-prime-minister-david-cameron-loses-parliamentary-vote-on-syrian-military-strike/2013/08/29/4fabb080-10f7-11e3-bdf6-e4fc677d94a1_story.html.

31. Polskie Radio, "US NATO Allies Snub Syria Military Action Call," August 30, 2013, at http://www.thenews.pl/1/10/Artykul/145799,US%E2%80%99s-NATO-allies-snub-Syria-military-action-call.

32. Scott Clement, "Most in US Oppose Syria Strike, *Post*–ABC Poll Finds," *Washington Post,* September 3, 2013, at http://www.washingtonpost.com/blogs/the-fix/wp/2013/09/03/most-in-u-s-oppose-syria-strike-post-abc-poll-finds/.

33. Richard C. Eichenberg, "Victory Has Many Friends: U.S. Public Opinion and the Use of Military Force, 1981–2005," *International Security* 30, no. 1 (2005): 140–77.

34. Carol J. Williams, "Pope Francis Condemns Chemical Weapons Use, Calls for Peace in Syria," *Los Angeles Times,* September 3, 2013, at http://articles.latimes.com/2013/sep/03/world/la-fg-wn-pope-francis-syria-peace-20130903.

35. Quoted in Kenneth B. Moss, *Undeclared War and the Future of U.S. Foreign Policy* (Baltimore: Johns Hopkins University Press, 2008), 50.

36. Cited in ibid.; see also Hendrickson, *The Clinton Wars,* 8.

37. Quoted in Louis Fisher, "Judicial Errors That Magnify Presidential Power," *The Federal Lawyer,* January–February 2014, 67–68.

38. Moss, *Undeclared War,* 72.

39. Nicole Duran, "Members' Libya Suit Dismissed Day of Qaddafi's Death," *National Journal,* October 21, 2011, at http://www.nationaljournal.com/nationalsecurity/members-libya-suit-dismissed-day-of-qaddafi-s-death-20111021.

40. Ryan C. Hendrickson, "Congress, War Powers, and the Judiciary: Restraining the Commander in Chief's Ability to Wage War," *Journal of African and International Law* 3, no. 3 (2010): 583–600.

41. James A. Baker III and Warren Christopher, "Put War Powers Back Where They Belong," *New York Times,* July 8, 2008; National War Powers Commission, *Final Report* (Charlottesville, Va.: Miller Center of Public Affairs, 2008).

42. U.S. House of Representatives, Committee on Foreign Affairs, *The Recommendations of the National War Powers Commission,* 111th Cong., 1st sess., March 5, 2009; U.S. Senate, Committee on Foreign Relations, *War Powers in the 21st Century,* 111th Cong., 1st sess., April 28, 2009.

43. Don Wolfensberger, "War Powers Proposal Gives the President Even More Authority," *Roll Call,* July 14, 2008, 9; Louis Fisher, "The Baker–Christopher War Powers Commission," *Presidential Studies Quarterly* 39, no. 1 (2009): 128–40; Michael J. Glennon, "The War Powers Resolution, Once Again," *American Journal of International Law* 103, no. 1 (2009): 75–82.

44. Kenneth P. Vogel, "Tea Party vs. Tea Party Caucus," *Politico,* August 2, 2010, at http://www.politico.com/news/stories/0810/40528.html.

45. Hendrickson, *The Clinton Wars,* 151, 167.

46. David M. Abshire, *Preventing World War III: A Realistic Grand Strategy* (New York: Harper & Row, 1988), 75–76.

47. John T. Shaw, "The Legacy of Senator Richard Lugar," *National Interest,* May 9, 2012, at http://nationalinterest.org/commentary/the-legacy-richard-lugar-6900.

48. Brien Hallett, *Declaring War: Congress, the President, and What the Constitution Does Not Say* (New York: Cambridge University Press, 2012), 237–40.

49. Hendrickson, *The Clinton Wars,* 34.

50. For more on Kucinich's views on the legality and constitutionality of an empowered commander in chief, see Dennis J. Kucinich, "The Seventh Annual Fritz B. Burns Lecture: The War Powers Resolution and Kosovo: The Power to Make War," *Loyola of Los Angeles Law Review* 34, no. 1 (2000): 61–69.

51. David S. Cloud, "Lawmaker Returns Home, a Hawk Turned War Foe," *New York Times,* November 22, 2005; David E. Sanger, "Iraq Dogs President as He Crosses Asia to Promote Trade," *New York Times,* November 18, 2005.

52. Thomas E. Ricks, *Fiasco: The American Military Adventure in Iraq* (New York: Penguin, 2007), 62–63.

53. David Gray Adler, "The Constitution and Presidential Warmaking: The Enduring Debate," *Political Science Quarterly* 103, no. 1 (1988): 1–36; Charles A. Lofgren, "War-Making under the Constitution: The Original Understanding," *Yale Law Journal* 81, no. 4 (1972): 672–702; Michael D. Ramsey, "Textualism and War Powers," *University of Chicago Law Review* 69, no. 4 (2002): 1543–1638.

54. Louis Fisher, *Presidential War Power,* 3rd ed. (Lawrence: University Press of Kansas, 2013); Francis D. Wormuth and Edwin B. Firmage, *To Chain the Dog of War: The War Power of Congress in History and Law,* 2nd ed. (Urbana: University of Illinois Press, 1989).

55. David Mitchell and Tansa George Massoud, "Anatomy of Failure: Bush's Decision-Making Process and the Iraq War," *Foreign Policy Analysis* 5, no. 3 (2009): 265–86; see also Lantis and Moskowitz, "Executive Decisions and Preventive War."

56. In *The Generals: American Military Command from World War II to Today* (New York: Penguin, 2012), Thomas E. Ricks provides a lengthy and compelling analysis of poor American generalship from the Korean War to the present time, with considerable attention devoted to the limitations evident in General Tommy Franks. For nearly identical arguments regarding General Franks, see Michael R. Gordon and Bernard E. Trainor, *Cobra II: The Inside Story of the Invasion and Occupation of Iraq* (New York: Vintage Books, 2007), and Andrew J. Bacevich, *The Limits of Power: The End of American Exceptionalism* (New York: Holt, 2008).

57. Hagel, with Kaminsky, *America,* 66.

58. Thomas E. Mann and Norman J. Ornstein, *The Broken Branch: How Congress Is Failing America and How to Get It Back on Track* (New York: Oxford University Press, 2006). For a more vitriolic summary of essentially the same argument, especially with regard to Congress's role in national-security affairs, see Bacevich, *The Limits of Power,* 69–70.

Selected Bibliography

Abramowitz, David. "The President, the Congress, and Use of Force: Legal and Political Considerations in Authorizing Use of Force against International Terrorism." *Harvard International Law Journal* 43, no. 1 (2002): 71–82.

Abshire, David M. *Preventing World War III: A Realistic Grand Strategy.* New York: Harper & Row, 1988.

Adam, Jeroen, Bruno Decordier, Kristof Titeca, and Koen Vlassenroot. "In the Name of the Father? Christian Militantism in Tripura, Northern Uganda, and Ambon." *Studies in Conflict and Terrorism* 30, no. 11 (2007): 963–83.

Adler, David Gray. "The Constitution and Presidential Warmaking: The Enduring Debate." *Political Science Quarterly* 103, no. 1 (1988): 1–36.

———. "The Law: George Bush as Commander in Chief: Toward the Nether World of Constitutionalism." *Presidential Studies Quarterly* 36, no. 3 (2006): 525–40.

Allen, Charles D. "Assessing the Army Profession." *Parameters* 41, no. 4 (2011): 73–86.

Arieff, Alexis, and Lauren Ploch. *The Lord's Resistance Army: The U.S. Response.* Washington, D.C.: Congressional Research Service, April 11, 2012.

Auerswald, David, and Forrest Matlzman. "Policymaking through Advice and Consent: Treaty Considerations by the United States Senate." *Journal of Politics* 65, no. 4 (2003): 1097–1110.

Bacevich, Andrew J. *The Limits of Power: The End of American Exceptionalism.* New York: Holt, 2008.

Barone, Michael, with Richard E. Cohen and Grant Ujifusa. *The Almanac of American Politics 2010.* Washington, D.C.: National Journal Group, 2009.

Berger, Matthew D. "Implementing a United Nations Security Council Resolution: The President's Power to Use Force with the Authorization of Congress." *Hastings International and Comparative Law Review* 15, no. 1 (1991): 83–109.

Biden, Joseph R., Jr., and John B. Ritch III. "The War Power at a Constitutional Impasse: A 'Joint Decision' Solution." *Georgetown Law Journal* 77, no. 1 (1988): 367–412.

Boylan, Timothy S., and Glenn A. Phelps. "The War Powers Resolution: A Rationale for Congressional Inaction." *Parameters* 31, no. 2 (2001): 109–24.

Branch, Adam. "Neither Peace nor Justice: Political Violence and Peasantry in Northern Uganda, 1986–1998." *African Studies Quarterly* 8, no. 2 (2005): 1–31.

Buchanan, Jessica, and Erik Landemalm, with Anthony Flacco. *Impossible Odds:*

The Kidnapping of Jessica Buchanan and Her Dramatic Rescue by Seal Team Six. New York: Atria Books, 2013.

Burden, Barry C. *Personal Roots of Representation.* Princeton, N.J.: Princeton University Press, 2007.

Carter, Ralph G., and James M. Scott. *Choosing to Lead: Understanding Congressional Foreign Policy Entrepreneurs.* Durham, N.C.: Duke University Press, 2009.

Carter, Ralph G., James M. Scott, and Charles M. Rowling. "Setting a Course: Congressional Foreign Policy Entrepreneurs in Post World War II U.S. Foreign Policy." *International Studies Perspectives* 5, no. 3 (2004): 278–99.

Cornelius, Erika N., and Ryan C. Hendrickson. "George W. Bush, War Powers, and U.N. Peacekeeping in Haiti." *White House Studies* 8, no. 1 (2008): 57–70.

Cox, Gary W., and William C. Terry. "Legislative Productivity in the 93d–105th Congresses." *Legislative Studies Quarterly* 33, no. 4 (2008): 603–18.

Cutrone, Ellen A., and Benjamin O. Fordham. "Commerce and Imagination: The Sources of Concern about International Human Rights in the US Congress." *International Studies Quarterly* 54, no. 3 (2010): 633–55.

Daalder, Ivo. *Getting to Dayton: The Making of America's Bosnia Policy.* Washington, D.C.: Brookings Institution Press, 2000.

Delaet, C. James, Charles M. Rowling, and James M. Scott. "Partisanship, Ideology, and Weapons of Mass Destruction in the Post–Cold War Congress: The Chemical Weapons and Comprehensive Test Ban Cases." *Illinois Political Science Review* 11, no. 1 (2007): 2–34.

Eichenberg, Richard C. "Victory Has Many Friends: U.S. Public Opinion and the Use of Military Force, 1981–2005." *International Security* 30, no. 1 (2005): 140–77.

Elsea, Jennifer K., and Richard F. Grimmett. *Declarations of War and Authorizations for the Use of Military Force: Historical Background and Legal Implications.* Washington, D.C.: Congressional Research Service, March 17, 2011.

Ely, John Hart. "Suppose Congress Wanted a War Powers Act That Worked." *Columbia Law Review* 88, no. 7 (1988): 1379–1431.

———. *War and Responsibility: Constitutional Lessons of Vietnam and Its Aftermath.* Princeton, N.J.: Princeton University Press, 1990.

The Federalist Papers. New York: New American Library, 1961.

Fisher, Louis. "The Baker–Christopher War Powers Commission." *Presidential Studies Quarterly* 39, no. 1 (2009): 128–40.

———. "Deciding on War against Iraq: Institutional Failures." *Political Science Quarterly* 118, no. 3 (2003): 389–410.

———. "Judicial Errors That Magnify Presidential Power." *The Federal Lawyer,* January–February 2014, 66–72.

———. "The Korean War: On What Legal Basis Did Truman Act?" *American Journal of International Law* 89, no. 1 (1995): 21–39.

———. "The Mexican War and Lincoln's 'Spot Resolutions.'" *Law Library of Congress,* August 19, 2009. At http://www.loufisher.org/docs/wi/433.pdf.

———. "Military Action against Iraq." *Presidential Studies Quarterly* 28, no. 4 (1998): 793–98.

———. "Military Operations in Libya: No War? No Hostilities?" *Presidential Studies Quarterly* 42, no. 1 (2012): 176–89.

———. "Parsing the War Power." *National Law Journal,* July 4, 2011, 50–51.

———. *Presidential War Power.* 3rd ed. Lawrence: University Press of Kansas, 2013.

———. "Sidestepping Congress: Presidents Acting under the UN and NATO." *Case Western Reserve Law Review* 47, no. 4 (1997): 1237–79.

Fisher, Louis, and David Gray Adler. "The War Powers Resolution: Time to Say Goodbye." *Political Science Quarterly* 113, no. 1 (1998): 1–20.

Forsythe, David P. *Human Rights in International Relations.* 3rd ed. Cambridge: Cambridge University Press, 2012.

———. *The Politics of International Law: U.S. Foreign Policy Reconsidered.* Boulder, Colo.: Lynne Rienner, 1990.

Gallis, Paul, and Vincent Morelli. *NATO in Afghanistan: A Test of the Transatlantic Alliance.* Washington, D.C.: Congressional Research Service, July 18, 2008.

Garrett, Nathan G. D., and Ryan C. Hendrickson. "NATO's Anti-piracy Operations: Strategic and Political Implications." *Atlantisch Perspectief* 33, no. 8 (2009): 9–13.

Gellman, Barton. *Angler: The Cheney Vice Presidency.* New York: Penguin, 2008.

Glennon, Michael J. *Constitutional Diplomacy.* Princeton, N.J.: Princeton University Press, 1990.

———. "The Constitution and Chapter VII of the United Nations Charter." *American Journal of International Law* 85, no. 1 (1991): 74–88.

———. "The Cost of 'Empty Words': A Comment on the Justice Department's Libya Opinion." Online feature. *Harvard National Security Journal,* April 14, 2011. At http://harvardnsj.org/2011/04/the-cost-of-empty-words-a-comment-on-the-justice-departments-libya-opinion/.

———. "Too Far Apart: The War Powers Resolution." *University of Miami Law Review* 50, no. 1 (1995): 17–31.

———. "United States Mutual Security Treaties: The Commitment Myth." *Columbia Journal of Transnational Law* 24, no. 3 (1986): 509–52.

———. "The War Powers Resolution, Once Again." *American Journal of International Law* 103, no. 1 (2009): 75–82.

Goldgeier, James M. *Not Whether but When: The U.S. Decision to Enlarge NATO.* Washington, D.C.: Brookings Institution Press, 1999.

Goldsmith, Jack. *Power and Constraint: The Accountable Presidency after 9/11.* New York: Norton, 2012.

Goldstein, Joel K. "The Rising Power of the Modern Vice Presidency." *Presidential Studies Quarterly* 38, no. 3 (2008): 374–89.

Golove, David. "From Versailles to San Francisco: The Revolutionary Transformation of the War Powers." *University of Colorado Law Review* 70, no. 4 (1999): 1491–1523.

Gordon, Michael R., and Bernard E. Trainor. *Cobra II: The Inside Story of the Invasion and Occupation of Iraq.* New York: Vintage Books, 2007.

Griffin, Stephen M. *Long Wars and the Constitution.* Cambridge, Mass.: Harvard University Press, 2013.

Haass, Richard N. "The Age of Nonpolarity." *Foreign Affairs* 87, no. 3 (2008): 44–56.

Hagel, Chuck, with Peter Kaminsky. *America: Our Next Chapter; Tough Questions, Straight Answers.* New York: HarperCollins, 2008.

Halberstam, David. *War in a Time of Peace: Bush, Clinton, and the Generals.* New York: Scribner's, 2001.

Hall, Brett M., Ryan C. Hendrickson, and Nathan M. Polak. "Diversionary American Military Actions? American Military Strikes on Grenada and Iraq." *Comparative Strategy* 32, no. 1 (2013): 35–51.

Hallett, Brien. "The 112th Congress, the War Powers Resolution, and the 2011 Libya Operation: A Normative Analysis of Functional and Organizational Incapacity." Paper presented at the Annual Meeting of the Western Political Science Association, March 22–24, 2012. At http://wpsa.research.pdx.edu/meet/2012/hallett.pdf.

———. *Declaring War: Congress, the President, and What the Constitution Does Not Say.* New York: Cambridge University Press, 2012.

Hammond, Susan Webb. *Congressional Caucuses in National Policy Making.* Baltimore: Johns Hopkins University Press, 1998.

Hendrickson, Ryan C. *The Clinton Wars: The Constitution, Congress, and War Powers.* Nashville: Vanderbilt University Press, 2002.

———. "Congress, War Powers, and the Judiciary: Restraining the Commander in Chief's Ability to Wage War." *Journal of African and International Law* 3, no. 3 (2010): 583–600.

Hendrickson, Ryan C., and Frédérick Gagnon. "The United States vs. Terrorism: Clinton, Bush, and Osama Bin Laden." In *Contemporary Cases in U.S. Foreign Policy: From Terrorism to Trade,* 3rd ed., edited by Ralph G. Carter, 1–24. Washington, D.C.: Congressional Quarterly Press, 2007.

Henehan, Marie. *Foreign Policy and Congress: An International Relations Perspective.* Ann Arbor: University of Michigan Press, 2000.

Henry, Donna H. "Notes: The War Powers Resolution, a Tool for Balancing Power through Negotiation." *Virginia Law Review* 70 (1984): 1037–58.

Hess, Gary R. "Presidents and the Congressional War Resolutions in 1991 and 2002." *Political Science Quarterly* 121, no. 1 (2006): 93–118.

Hibbing, John R. *Congressional Careers: Contours of Life in the U.S. House of Representatives.* Chapel Hill: University of North Carolina Press, 1991.

Howell, William G., and Jon C. Pevehouse. "When Congress Stops Wars." *Foreign Affairs* 86, no. 5 (2007): 95–107.

———. *While Dangers Gather: Congressional Checks on Presidential War Powers.* Princeton, N.J.: Princeton University Press, 2007.

Johnson, Robert David. *Congress and the Cold War.* New York: Cambridge University Press, 2006.

Kaplan, Lawrence S. *The United States and NATO: The Formative Years.* Lexington: University Press of Kentucky, 1984.

Kassop, Nancy. "The War Power and Its Limits." *Presidential Studies Quarterly* 33, no. 3 (2003): 509–29.

Katzmann, Robert A. "War Powers: Toward a New Accommodation." In *A Question of Balance: The President, the Congress, and Foreign Policy,* edited by Thomas E. Mann, 35–69. Washington, D.C.: Brookings Institution Press, 1990.

Keynes, Edward. "The War Powers Resolution: A Bad Idea Whose Time Has Come and Gone." *University of Toledo Law Review* 23, no. 2 (1992): 343–62.

Koh, Harold Hongju. *National Security Constitution: Sharing Power after the Iran–Contra Affair.* New Haven, Conn.: Yale University Press, 1990.

Kohn, Richard. "The Erosion of Civilian Control of the Military in the United States Today." *Naval War College Review* 55, no. 3 (2002): 9–59.

Kraska, James. "Coalition Strategy and the Pirates of the Gulf of Aden and the Red Sea." *Comparative Strategy* 28, no. 3 (2009): 197–216.

Krotoski, Mark L. "Essential Elements of Reform of the War Powers Resolution." *Santa Clara Law Review* 29, no. 3 (1989): 607–752.

Kucinich, Dennis J. "The Seventh Annual Fritz B. Burns Lecture: The War Powers Resolution and Kosovo: The Power to Make War." *Loyola of Los Angeles Law Review* 34, no. 1 (2000): 61–69.

Lantis, Jeffrey S., and Eric Moskowitz. "Executive Decisions and Preventive War: Strategies of Intervention and Withdrawal in Iraq (2003–2011)." In *Contemporary Cases in U.S. Foreign Policy: From Terrorism to Trade,* 5th ed., edited by Ralph G. Carter, 66–99. Washington, D.C.: Congressional Quarterly Press, 2014.

Lehr, Peter. "Maritime Piracy as a U.S. Foreign Policy Problem: The Case of the *Maersk Alabama.*" In *Contemporary Cases in U.S. Foreign Policy: From Terrorism to Trade,* 4th ed., edited by Ralph G. Carter, 200–228. Washington, D.C.: Congressional Quarterly Press, 2011.

Lofgren, Charles A. "War-Making under the Constitution: The Original Understanding." *Yale Law Journal* 81, no. 4 (1972): 672–702.

Madison, James. *Notes of Debates in the Federal Convention of 1787 Reported by James Madison.* 1966. Reprint. New York: Norton, 1987.

Mann, Thomas E., and Norman J. Ornstein. *The Broken Branch: How Congress Is Failing America and How to Get It Back on Track.* New York: Oxford University Press, 2006.

Marshall, Bryan W., and Brandon C. Prins. "The Pendulum of Congressional Power: Agenda Change, Partisanship, and Demise of Post–World War II Foreign Policy Consensus." *Congress and the Presidency* 29, no. 2 (2002): 195–212.

Mayhew, David. *Congress: The Electoral Connection.* New Haven, Conn.: Yale University Press, 1974.

McCormick, James M., and Neil J. Mitchell. "Commitments, Transnational Interests, and Congress: Who Joins the Congressional Human Rights Caucus?" *Political Research Quarterly* 60, no. 4 (2007): 579–92.

McHugh, Kelly. "Understanding Congress's Role in Terminating Unpopular Wars: A Comparison of the Vietnam and Iraq Wars." *Democracy and Security* 10, no. 3 (2014): 191–224.

McKay, Susan. "Girls as 'Weapons of Terror' in Northern Uganda and Sierra Leone Rebel Fighting Forces." *Studies in Conflict and Terrorism* 28, no. 5 (2005): 385–97.

Mitchell, David, and Tansa George Massoud. "Anatomy of Failure: Bush's Decision-Making Process and the Iraq War." *Foreign Policy Analysis* 5, no. 3 (2009): 265–86.

Montgomery, Bruce P. "Congressional Oversight: Vice President Richard B. Cheney's Executive Branch Triumph." *Political Science Quarterly* 120, no. 4 (2005–2006): 581–617.

Moss, Kenneth B. *Undeclared War and the Future of U.S. Foreign Policy.* Baltimore: Johns Hopkins University Press, 2008.

National War Powers Commission. *Final Report.* Charlottesville, Va.: Miller Center of Public Affairs, 2008.

Pham, J. Peter. "Anti-piracy, Adrift." *Journal of International Security Affairs* 18, no. 1 (2010). At http://www.securityaffairs.org/issues/2010/18/pham.php.

Ploch, Lauren, Christopher M. Blanchard, Ronald O'Rourke, R. Chuck Mason, and Rawle O. King. *Piracy off the Horn of Africa.* Washington, D.C.: Congressional Research Service, April 27, 2011.

Prendergast, John, with Don Cheadle. *The Enough Movement: Fighting to End Africa's Worst Human Rights Crimes.* New York: Three Rivers Press, 2010.

Ramsey, Michael D. "Textualism and War Powers." *University of Chicago Law Review* 69, no. 4 (2002): 1543–1638.

Ricks, Thomas E. *Fiasco: The American Military Adventure in Iraq.* New York: Penguin, 2007.

———. *The Gamble: General David Petraeus and the American Military Adventure in Iraq, 2006–2008.* New York: Penguin, 2009.

———. *The Generals: American Military Command from World War II to Today.* New York: Penguin, 2012.

Rubenzer, Trevor. "Campaign Contributions and US Foreign Policy Outcomes: An Analysis of Cuban-American Interests." *American Journal of Political Science* 55, no. 1 (2011): 105–16.

Rubner, Michael. "The Reagan Administration, the 1973 War Powers Resolution, and the Invasion of Grenada." *Political Science Quarterly* 100, no. 4 (1985–1986): 627–47.

Rupp, Richard E. *NATO after 9/11: An Alliance in Continuing Decline.* New York: Palgrave, 2006.

Sanger, David E. *Confront and Conceal: Obama's Secret Wars and Surprising Use of American Power.* New York: Crown, 2012.

Schonberg, Karl K. "Global Security and Legal Restraint: Reconsidering War Powers after September 11." *Political Science Quarterly* 119, no. 1 (2004): 115–42.

Shultz, George P. *Turmoil and Triumph: My Years as Secretary of State.* New York: Scribner's, 1993.

Silverstein, Gordon. *Imbalance of Powers: Constitutional Interpretation and the Making of American Foreign Policy.* New York: Oxford University Press, 1997.

Sofaer, Abram. *War, Foreign Affairs, and Constitutional Power: The Origins.* Cambridge, U.K.: Ballinger, 1976.

Souva, Mark, and David Rohde. "Elite Differences and Partisanship in Congressional Foreign Policy, 1975–1996." *Political Research Quarterly* 60, no. 1 (2007): 113–23.

Suhrke, Astri. "A Contradictory Mission? Stabilization to Combat in Afghanistan." *International Peacekeeping* 15, no. 2 (2008): 214–36.

Symonds, Craig L. *Navalists and Antinavalists: The Naval Policy Debate in the United States, 1785–1827.* Newark: University of Delaware Press, 1980.

Tower, John. "Congress versus the President: The Formulation and Implementation of American Foreign Policy." *Foreign Affairs* 60, no. 2 (1981): 229–46.

Turner, Robert F. *Repealing the War Powers Resolution.* Washington, D.C.: Brassey's, 1991.

Vinci, Anthony. "The Strategic Use of Fear by the Lord's Resistance Army." *Small Wars and Insurgencies* 16, no. 3 (2005): 360–81.

Warburg, Gerald. "Congress: Checking Presidential Power." In *The National Security Enterprise: Navigating the Labyrinth,* edited by Roger Z. George and Harvey Rishikof, 227–46. Washington, D.C.: Georgetown University Press, 2011.

Weissman, Stephen R. *A Culture of Deference: Congress's Failure of Leadership in Foreign Policy.* New York: Basic Books, 1995.

Wolfensberger, Don. "War Powers Proposal Gives the President Even More Authority." *Roll Call,* July 14, 2008, 8–9.

Wombwell, James A. *The Long War against Piracy: Historical Trends.* Occasional Paper no. 32. Ft. Leavenworth, Kans.: Combat Studies Institute Press, 2010.

Wormuth, Francis D., and Edwin B. Firmage. *To Chain the Dog of War: The War Power of Congress in History and Law.* 2nd ed. Urbana: University of Illinois Press, 1989.

Yoo, John. *The Powers of War and Peace: The Constitution and Foreign Affairs after 9/11.* Chicago: University of Chicago Press, 2005.

Zeisberg, Mariah. *War Powers: The Politics of Constitutional Authority.* Princeton, N.J.: Princeton University Press, 2013.

Zenko, Micah. *Reforming U.S. Drone Strike Policies.* Special Report no. 65. New York: Council on Foreign Relations, January 2013.

Zunes, Stephen, and Ben Terrall. "East Timor: Reluctant Support for Self-Determination." In *Contemporary Cases in U.S. Foreign Policy,* edited by Ralph G. Carter, 1–30. Washington, D.C.: Congressional Quarterly Press, 2002.

Index

BOOKS IN THE SERIES

The Gulf: The Bush Presidencies and the Middle East
Michael F. Cairo

Diplomatic Games: Sport, Statecraft, and International Relations since 1945
Edited by Heather L. Dichter and Andrew L. Johns

CPSIA information can be obtained at www.ICGtesting.com
Printed in the USA
BVOW04*0047040515

398647BV00002B/3/P

9 780813 160948